CABBAGES & ROSES

# home-made
# VINTAGE

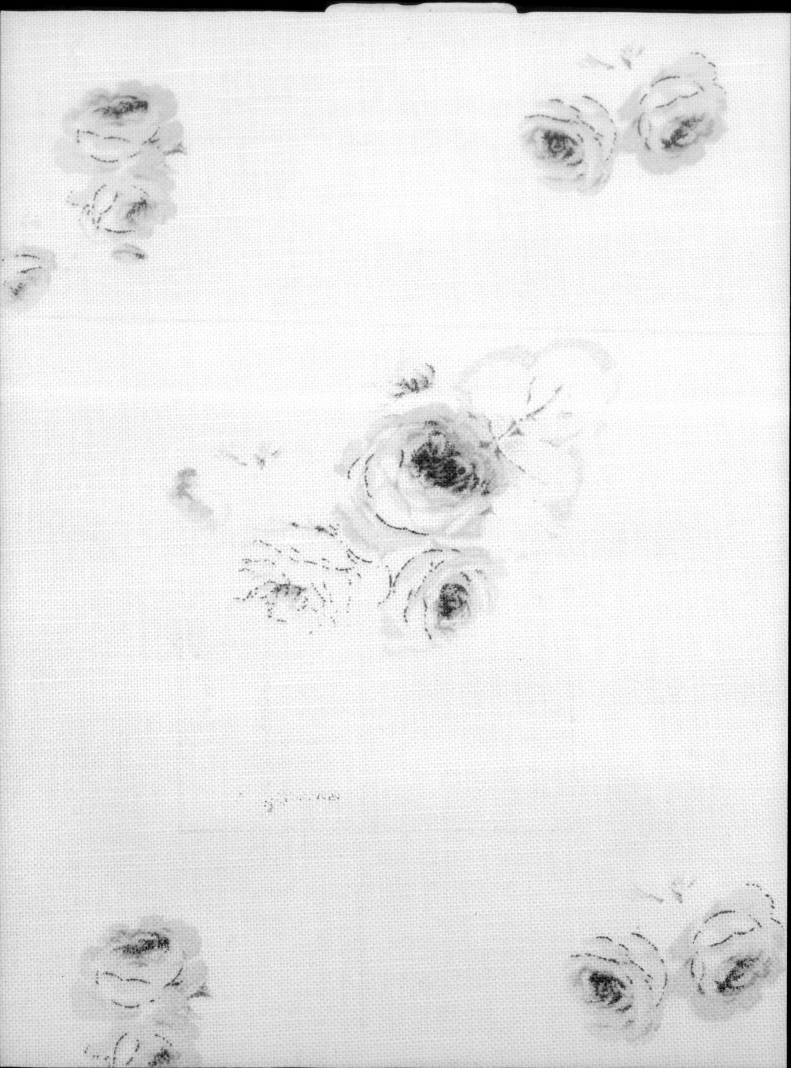

CABBAGES & ROSES

# home-made
# VINTAGE

CHRISTINA STRUTT

CICO BOOKS

LONDON NEW YORK

First edition published in 2006 by CICO Books
This paperback edition published in 2009
an imprint of Ryland Peters & Small Ltd
20–21 Jockey's Fields, London WC1R 4BW

www.cicobooks.co.uk

10 9 8 7 6 5

A CIP catalogue record for this book is available from the
British Library.

ISBN-13: 978 1 906525 71 2

Printed in China

Editor: Gillian Haslam
Designer: Christine Wood
Photographer: Lucinda Symons
Stylist: Christina Strutt
Sewing instructions: Jane Bolsover
Illustrations: Kate Simunek

# contents

# introduction

Somewhere along the line, we seem to have lost the knack of making. It is so much simpler to buy, with huge chain stores supplying everything we could possibly want for less money than we could possibly make it for. We all have so much, but we all have so much of the same. It is almost impossible to buy a gift without suspecting that the recipient already has one—even if they live on the opposite side of the country, or the other side of the world, it is quite likely that they have the same shops, selling the same things.

Our passion for vintage clothing and charity shops is satisfying the need to own something different. Dressing in vintage clothing is one way of guaranteeing that you will never stumble upon your clone. But, like all fashions, vintage and hand-made originals are a limited resource. So our only real option is to create our own generation of unique, handmade pieces.

It has been a great pleasure putting this book together. However, in the beginning, when the subject was suggested to me I was reluctant, even petulant—the thought of all that sewing did not initially appeal. However, my publisher was most persuasive, and eventually the thought dawned on me, how hard can it be?

I should point out that because I could not possibly sew everything myself within the time allowed, I had every intention of recruiting sewing volunteers to assist me. This would not have been a problem had I not been rather casual about timing. During the Christmas holidays, when diary dates, deadlines, and January seem such a long way off, I was caught unaware. I was faced with a sewing machine but I hadn't a clue how to thread or operate it. When that hurdle had been overcome with the help of my friend Tina Wright who had once been a machinist, I bent the only needle I had. The situation was getting out of hand and I was almost ready to give up. However, my refrain in life, when faced with impossible situations (income tax forms, flat tires, tangled tree lights, financial reports), is "How hard can it be?". I only have to say those five words to myself to stop, gather my thoughts, concentrate, take a deep breath, and face things one step at a time. I whizzed into my local sewing machine shop, learned how to replace the needle, bought ten more, and set to work.

*create your own unique*
*hand-made pieces*

# *my passion is*
## *to make things beautiful*

So new are my sewing skills, and so limited my time, it would be unfair and untrue to claim that I had made everything in this book. My mother Mary Amoroso-Centeno and my friend Penny Menato, who makes many of the home wares for Cabbages & Roses, stepped into the breach and helped with the actual sewing of my designs, but I'm proud of the fact that my stitching skills improved and I made many of the items myself. This is proof that the projects I have chosen are so simple, even I can make them!

My working life requires a hodge-podge of skills. I design clothes, home wares, and dress shops, I style photographs, decorate houses, make books, buy antiques and vintage clothing for

### *the charm of home-made gifts*

our shops, read (and try to understand) financial reports. My true passion, however, is to make things as beautiful as I am able. The less promise a situation has, the more I enjoy the challenge—give me an empty space and no budget and I can perform wonders.

Throughout the pages of this book there are beautiful photographs of very simple things, and my aim is to explain what to make, and what to make it out of, as well as how to make it. Especially important is the uniqueness of the home made, the wholesome satisfaction, the sense of wellbeing and achievement that completing a project yourself brings. I have been a lifelong hoarder of buttons, scraps of fabrics, beads, string, ribbon, boxes, bags, shrunken cardigans, accidentally boiled wool, linen sheets—the list is endless. Apart from the environmentally sound aspect of mending and making do, the charm of homemade gifts, clothes, and accessories is something that is hard to better.

Nothing passes through my life without my hoarding instinct pushing its way to the fore. Junk stores, charity shops, and markets cannot be bypassed without inspection. If a pretty fabric has been made into a horrendous dress, the dress must be bought. The horrid bag saved by a charming lining can be taken apart. The dress could become cushions, pillows, lavender sachets, Christmas cards, or patches on anything, including patchworks, napkins, a tiny curtain for a beach house, a book cover. The buttons on the dress will go into the button jar, the zipper into the emergency zipper bag. Several pieces of dress can even be made into table covering if you follow the project featured on page 16.

*the longer you keep it,
the more desirable it
will become*

The same applies to any fabric, piece of clothing, or old curtain. The longer you keep it, the more desirable it will become—one day, for sure, it will come in handy. More robust fabrics such as tweed jackets, overcoats, blankets, and quilts can also be doctored or transformed. Blankets can make draft-proof curtains, or can act as lining for thinner curtain fabric. Making blanket patchworks could be an amusing diversion during the winter months, and you will be guaranteed a warm lap for the duration. Tweed jackets are a passion of mine—the old ones have good shapes and were made so well. If they are too big for you, consider washing them in a hot wash—this will shrink them and give them a vintage time-worn look. This, however, must be done with care and can either completely ruin the garment or make it a perfect fit.

The disastrous incident recounted on page 79 with my very new, very beautiful hand-knitted Fair Isle sweater, although heartbreaking, has triumphantly been turned into an amusing set of pencil pots. Although I do not recommend purposely washing something of great beauty and with useful function (as I did by accident), washing wool in extremely hot water is a method of felting which is useful to know. The stiff, unfrayable nature of the wool gives you a whole new medium to play with. It is also very sturdy and would happily make small or large bags depending on the size of the sweater. Hot water bottle covers, Christmas decorations (especially good when made from bright red sweaters), slippers, and book covers can all be made from felt. A patchwork of felted wool in interesting shapes can become a beautiful work of art. Felt can also be used for monogrammed items, binding, hems or lengthening skirts, dresses, or sleeves.

Look at knitwear in a second-hand shop in a new light. Bear in mind that you can take it home and wash it to transform it into a new "fabric." However, I must stress that felting wool does not always work so perfectly when you intend to do it—it usually only happens when you don't want it to. To felt a sweater, make sure it is 100 percent wool (any manmade fibers will prevent the felting process). Put into the washing machine set on the highest temperature setting, then dry your new, stiff little garment flat.

## *display your collections*

In order that your life and home does not become a magpie's nest of chaos, create order in the hoarding department and find a lovely way to store or even display your collections whilst they wait to be transformed into something useful. I love my shelves when the fabrics have been neatly folded and arranged in color order, but all too soon they become unruly. I always mean to tie them in neat, color-coordinated bundles with string or satin ribbons, but I always seem to become distracted by another chore.

If you come across lovely sets of boxes in a market or junk shop, consider them an orderly method of storing buttons or lengths of ribbon. Stick a sample on the outside so you don't need to open every box to find the right color. Jam or jelly jars (especially those with cheery printed gingham lids) are also an ideal way to keep buttons, sea shells, or tiny reels of thread in order.

In short, throw nothing away without considering its future usefulness and discover the pleasure in the home made. I hope that even if you have never made anything in your life before, you will now do so.

*Christina Strutt*

living room

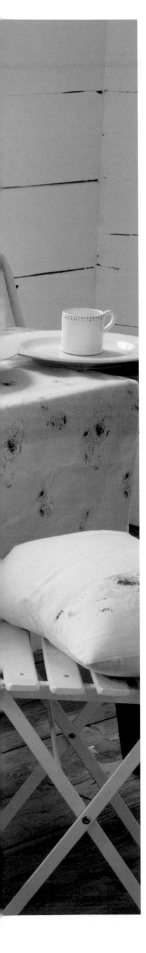

## tied tablecloth and drawn thread napkin ring

This tablecloth is a very clever way of making something out of relatively small pieces of fabric. For a large gathering when you need an unusually long table and never have a tablecloth large enough to cover it, this cloth is the perfect solution.

These charming napkin rings feature delicate drawn thread work, which you could also use on the napkins if you wished. You will need to find linen fabric with a fairly loose weave so the threads can easily be extracted.

Sometimes you can buy fabric remainders or ends of lines from fabric shops very cheaply—these would be ideal for the tablecloth. The fabrics do not necessarily need to be the same or even match—a hodge podge of fabrics tied together down the center of a long table can be extremely fetching. Try using different tartans tied together along a table for New Year celebrations. Lengths of antique linen sheets can be cut up hemmed and tied together, or red and white fabrics used alternately can be visually striking for Thanksgiving.

*try using several mismatching fabrics*

*See page 84 for the tablecloth instructions and page 86 for the drawn thread napkin ring instructions.*

*add an elegant touch to any dining table*

## linen easy-sew curtain

These extremely clever curtain poles with small clips attached to the curtain rings provide endless possibilities for changing curtains quickly and easily.

The most beautiful, versatile, and elegant fabric to use is an antique French linen sheet which, although they are becoming more difficult to source, are extremely simple to use as there is no sewing involved at all. At Cabbages & Roses we handprint some of our beautiful fabric designs onto antique linen sheets and these can become the ultimate in simple readymade curtains. If using other fabrics, all you have to do is hem them first.

Blankets can also be used in this way, and these are particularly useful if you need a curtain to prevent drafts in front of doors or between rooms or to curtain off a drafty passageway. Just make sure that the clips are strong enough to hold a heavier fabric.

*See page 90 for curtain instructions.*

*bring a vintage look to your living room*

## contrasting tie-top curtains

This is another project that can give instant satisfaction. Here I have used contrasting fabric on the back and front of these curtains, so you can swap which side of the curtain faces into the room for a different look.

Attaching ties at the top of the panels is a very simple solution for hanging and looks more informal than using curtain tape. If you wish, you could use ribbon instead of making ties. There are many variations to this project, so experiment with plain calico and tape ties, tartan blankets tied with velvet ribbon for warm winter drapes, quilts tied with satin ribbon, or fine floaty muslin tied with voile ribbons in the summer months.

*See page 93 for curtain instructions.*

### door curtains
If making door curtains, it is a good idea to make them overlong so that they "puddle" on the floor and prevent any drafts creeping under the door.

# dress your lampshade with pretty fabric covers

## lampshade cover

Covering a plain lampshade with a pretty fabric lampshade dress can add the perfect finishing touch to a room, bringing the whole scheme together. It is an ideal project to use up fabric leftover from making other furnishings for the room, such as curtains, pillows, or slipcovers. It is also a way to make a change for little effort—something that always pleases me.

If you change your furnishings according to the seasons, you can make several lampshade dresses to coordinate either with heavy winter drapes, or with lightweight summer fabrics. These covers can also be used over glass ceiling shades.

*See page 92 for lampshade instructions.*

# cupboard door panel

Simplicity itself: these cupboard door panels are a wonderful way of changing the entire look of a room with little effort. Of course you need to start with doors with open panels, but it is not difficult to remove the original wooden panels and fit rectangles of chicken wire to the fronts in their place, to create a traditional French country look (the chicken wire can be tacked to the rear of the door; bend back any sharp edges). Be careful to use chicken wire that will not rust, as paint can effect the metal—when buying the wire, explain the end use to ensure you are sold the correct type.

## to make the panels

To make the panels, measure width and depth of your cupboard "window." Add 5½ in. (14cm) to both the width and depth measurements for hems, then cut out a rectangle of fabric to this size. Press and stitch a double-turned ¾ in. (2cm) hem around all edges. Stitch the looped side of some Velcro tape to the top and bottom hems. Stick the hooked side of the tape to the cupboard door to correspond. Press the tapes together to fix the curtain in place.

*a bold, contemporary approach to traditional monograms*

## monogrammed pillow

This is a wonderful way to personalize a handmade pillow cover. A monogrammed item is very special and makes a thoughtful gift that will be treasured. Use the initials of the recipient or an anniversary date. You can adapt this idea for use on many other household items—a duvet cover, a baby's blanket, even a dog blanket! Of course whole words can be used, but the letters should be scaled down accordingly.

The easiest way to obtain letters is from your computer—scale up the required initials, print and cut out, and use these as your template. Felt is the easiest fabric to use as it does not fray, but the color could run in the wash—see the notes in the step-by-step instructions for laundering.

*See page 85 for pillow instructions.*

# chair slipcover

If, like me, you find your home is filled with fleamarket treasures, here's a simple idea for bringing a collection of chairs together with a uniform look. These pretty slipcovers are easier to make than more formal, fitted slipcovers, and the dimensions can easily be adjusted to suit different chair sizes. A simple fabric "envelope" covers the chair back, while a seat pillow covered in the same fabric neatens the whole scheme.

As an alternative, the seat pillow can be made on its own, with fabric ties stitched to two corners, to attach the pad to the chair (see facing page).

*See page 102 for the slipcover instructions.*

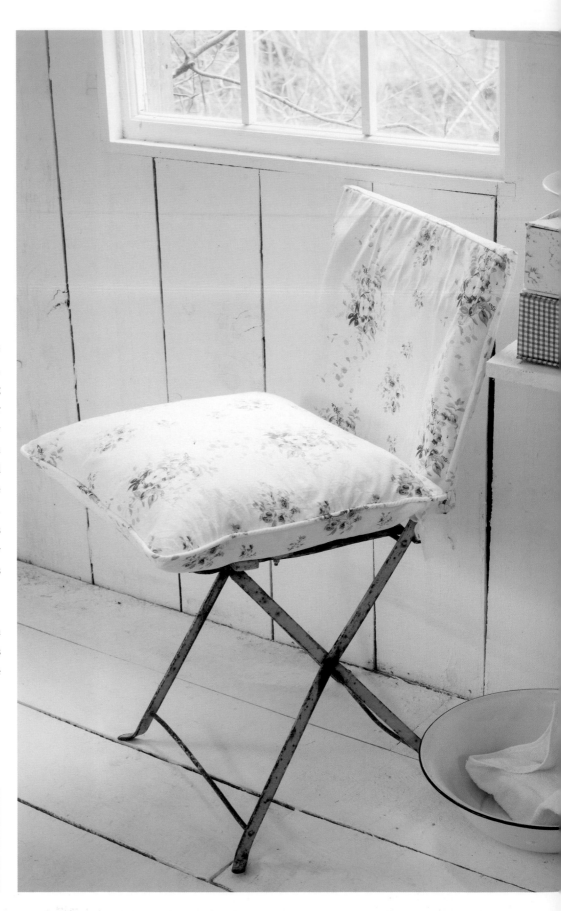

### for extra comfort
If you wish, you could also add a layer of padding or batting to the slipcover, to soften the back of the chair.

*give flea market finds
a fresh look*

# bedroom
# and bathroom

## muslin canopy

*for romantic
summer nights, dress
the bed in muslin*

Although only tropical climates are plagued by mosquitoes and require mosquito nets for purely practical reasons, the idea of a bed swathed in lengths of beautiful muslin is such a romantic notion that I have dressed one of the beds in my house in this way. Here, in the simplest of bedrooms, white furniture, walls, and floor contrast with the drama of printed muslin or netting for the ultimate in finishing touches. Choose a fine fabric that will let sunlight gently filter through, and match it to the bed linen. The fabric drapes gently over a circular hoop which is attached to the ceiling beam with a fabric loop.

*See page 94 for the muslin canopy instructions.*

# bolster pillow

It is my belief that you can never have enough pillows either on a sofa or a bed, and this bolster is particularly suitable for a bedroom. Making the cover is a little more involved than some of the other pillow projects in this book, but it is well worth the effort. The cover fits snugly around the pillow form and the neatly tailored ends are finished with a matching button.

A simpler way to make a bolster cover is simply to wrap fabric tightly around the pillow form and slipstitch the join. Gather the ends together and tie with a length of ribbon.

*See page 104 for bolster pillow instructions.*

## fabric-covered headboards

These fabric headboards are the easiest thing in the world to make. All you need for this simple design is a little fabric, some batting, and a staple gun. These are very straightforward to create, so it's easy to change your headboard on a whim. It's best to start off with partly upholstered headboards, similar to those shown here.

*update headboards to match your bed linen*

### to cover the headboard

Take a large sheet of paper and trace around the edge of the padded section on the headboard. Use the tracing to cut out a new fabric cover adding 1 in. (2.5cm) all around for hems. Fold over and pin hems in place. Starting at the center top and using a staple gun, begin to fasten the fabric to the very edge of the pad. Work outward, stapling on alternate sides, pulling the fabric smooth and taut as you go. To finish, cover the staples around the edge of the pad by gluing on a matching braid or tape.

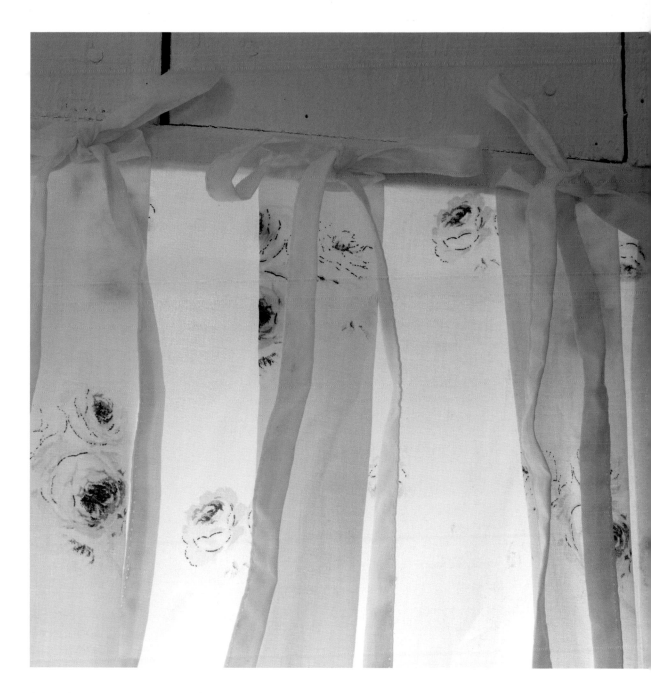

# bedroom curtains

Here's another style of tie-top curtains which are more detailed than those shown on page 20. This design incorporates a pleat heading, which gives a similar appearance to that achieved when curtain header tape is used. This style is really only suitable for unlined cotton curtains.

All tie-top curtains could be easily used on a shower curtain rail in front of the plastic waterproof curtain, making for a much prettier and more feminine look.

*See page 95 for curtain instructions.*

# bunting

Bunting is one of the cheeriest of adornments—a celebration in itself. When we first launched Cabbages and Roses, my friend and partner Brigette Buchanan made bunting washing lines to sell. Since then, I have made strings of bunting to hang indoors and in the garden.

This project is a fun way to use up small pieces of fabric leftover from other projects. You can either opt for a simple color scheme to tie in with other furnishings in the room, as in the pretty red and white fabrics used here, or mix-and-match a vibrant multi-color scheme, using up any fabric remainders you have in your sewing basket.

### how to make the bunting

Using a pair of pinking shears, cut out 9 in. (23cm) squares from printed cotton fabrics. Fold the squares diagonally over a length of cord or cotton tape, and stitch them in place with a running stitch. Tie the ends of the line to ceiling rafters or fasten them high up on the walls to decorate a bedroom.

## hot water bottle cover

There is something so comforting about a hot water bottle, whether used to soothe sore muscles or as an easy way to warm up on a chilly evening.

For this project use any fabric with a soft or luxurious feel. Soft cotton has been used here, but terry cloth, velvet, cashmere, or felted wool would work equally well—in fact, anything provided it is not a manmade fabric. Here I have used a contrasting fabric for the lining, but if you are in a hurry, you can omit the lining as long as the inside seams are neat.

*See page 96 for hot water bottle cover instructions.*

# *warm and cozy bedtimes are something to look forward to*

## tied pillow cover

These pretty square pillows in contrasting fabrics are just the ticket for propping up in bed on a lazy Sunday morning. When it comes to sewing, I'm all in favor of simplicity, so these pillow covers are tied together with bows rather than having a zipper fastening, making them one of the simplest projects to make.

As shown here, you can use two different types of fabric—using complementary colorways of the same pattern always looks very effective. And if you wish to make the project even simpler, you could use ribbon in a coordinating color for the two sets of ties, rather than making them from matching fabric.

*See page 98 for pillow cover instructions.*

# bed skirt

Although you can buy readymade bed skirts, it is sometimes rather nice to be able to incorporate a fabric that ties together the whole scheme of a room. Here I have used a soft pink checked fabric, which adds some strength to the soft pastel colors of the bedroom. The added bonus of using a checked or striped fabric is that the printed lines make for easier cutting and hemming.

*See page 100 for the bed skirt instructions.*

### to make fabric go further

I have used an old sheet for the area that sits under the mattress and simply stitched the bed skirt to the outside of it. This means you can afford to indulge in a more luxurious fabric if you wish, as you only need enough for the areas on view.

# lavender pillow pocket

This is a charming addition to a pillow—a small pocket to scent the pillowcase with the sleep-inducing perfume of lavender. Although it looks delightful filled with lavender flowers, it may be more practical to sew a tiny sachet, fill it with dried lavender, and tuck this inside the pillow pocket. You could also use the pocket to hold a lace-edged handkerchief, or fabric sachets filled with rose petals. This idea could be used on children's pillowcases for a gift from the tooth fairy. Stitch the pocket toward the top of the pillowcase to provide easy access for the fairy!

*See page 113 for the pocket instructions.*

*for sweetly scented dreams*

*travel in style*
*with matching*
*accessories*

## matching shoe bag and jewelry case

When traveling with stylish friends, one of the many things that set them apart from me and my luggage is that they remember to pack their shoes in neat little shoe bags. Mine are inevitably wrapped in plastic grocery bags—and that's if I'm clever enough to remember to pack my favorite shoes in the first place. My idea of sheer luxury would be to own enough shoe bags to decant all my shoes, whether traveling or not—how divine a neat line of shoe bags would be, rather than a random pile carelessly stowed in a closet.

And to continue my quest for elegant travel, I've made a drawstring jewelry case to match my shoe bags. You could even scale down the jewelry case to make a smaller version for storing cosmetics.

*See page 106 for shoe bag instructions and page 108 for jewelry case instructions.*

# zippered cosmetic case

I love the idea of being able to make cosmetic cases—they are such a perfect gift, and I love owning them. I have four on the go at the moment and nothing gives me more pleasure than packing a new one for a special trip.

When traveling I like to keep large items that may leak in one bag in the suitcase and smaller items in a purse-sized bag to be kept with me at all times. I have suffered the loss of a suitcase and know how inconsolable I am without my essential face creams and emergency medicines. You could make a matching set by scaling up the measurements given for this project.

*See page 110 for cosmetic case instructions.*

*See page 110 for cosmetic case instructions.*

### choosing fabrics

This bag is made from cotton with a separate waterproof lining, but you could make it in a single layer of sturdy cotton for hairbrushes and combs, and items that won't leak.

## laundry bags

I love the concept of the laundry bag. Why not make one for each member of the family, to hang in the bathroom or bedroom, ready to receive dirty laundry? Taking the concept to extremes or to an easy conclusion, depending on your point of view, you could have laundry bags to receive white clothes, colored clothes, hand-washable items, and so on. This way, they can be merely emptied into the machine without having to be sorted out.

If you wish, you could stitch monogram initials to each bag to identify the family member it belongs to, or give each person bags in different fabrics or colors.

*See page 112 for laundry bag instructions.*

*bring fresh, pretty order to laundry day*

## *perfect for creating privacy*

## café curtains

Curtains that just cover the lower half of a window are great for screening small or unusually shaped windows, such as in a bathroom. Here I have used dish towels for these curtains, but any lightweight cotton fabric will work, especially checked fabric. The beauty of using dish towels is that they do not need hemming.

*for a comfortable breakfast in bed, pad the curtain with a soft, thick fabric*

You can also adapt the project for use in a bedroom. If a bed does not have a headboard, you can make a decorative curtain along the same lines as the café curtains. This is especially effective in children's rooms where it is useful to be able to change the curtains. If you wish, you could pad the curtain with soft, thick lining or batting to provide a softer, more comfortable surface to lean against when reading late at night or enjoying breakfast in bed.

*See page 91 for curtain instructions.*

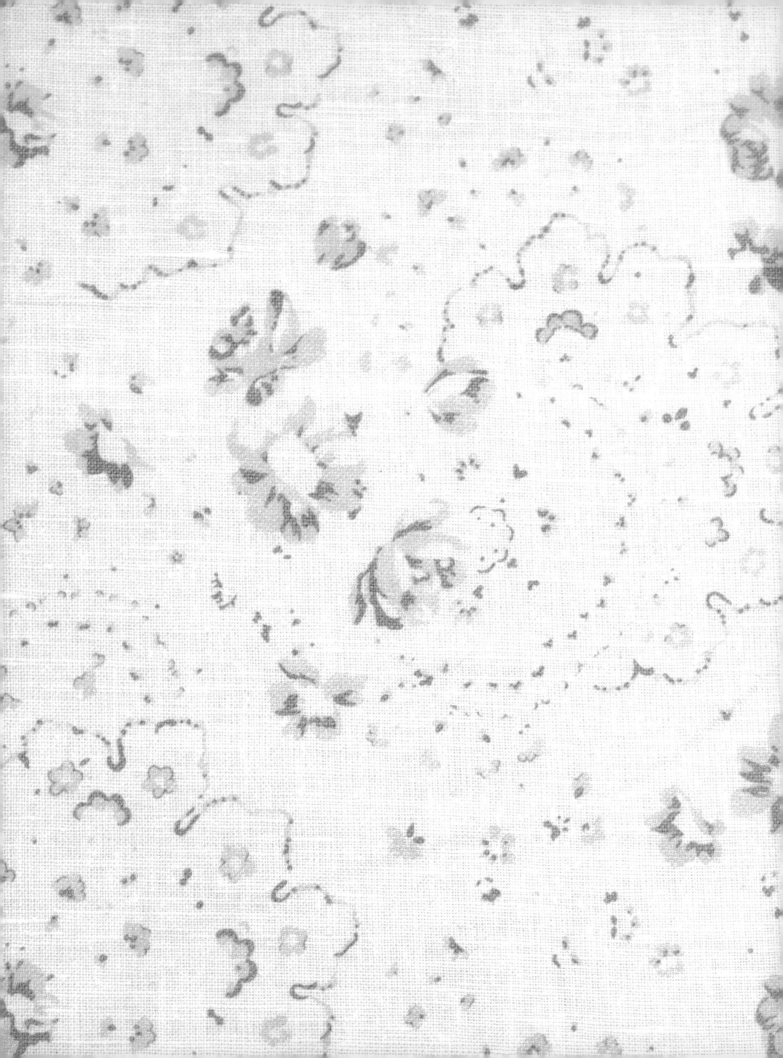

clothes and
accessories

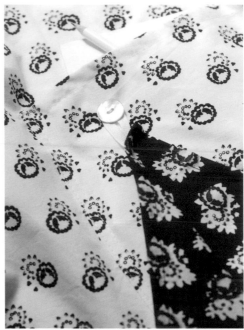

*housework becomes less of a chore with these stylish aprons*

## kitchen aprons

I find that the moment I put on an apron, I become a different person—cheerful and more organized. I feel I want to cook or make things or clean. It seems to bring me a new wholesome energy—others, apparently, feel the same way!

This apron is a particularly good shape and fits all sizes. It can be worn with the bib around the neck, or folded down for a half apron. The long ties gather the apron close to your body for streamlined efficiency! I always find myself drying my hands on my apron, so this design features a separate dish towel attached to the apron with a button and loop for just this purpose.

*See page 114 for the apron instructions.*

## fabric brooch

This project shows how fun and easy it can be to customize a tweed jacket. The brooch can be made from all manner of odds and ends found in the sewing box. If you start a regime of never throwing anything away and store extraordinary scraps, there is no end to the variety of brooches that you can make. The smallest pieces of braid, ribbon, and fabric can be used. Be careful not to be too precise and predictable, and search out the unexpected—try using small coins, woven lettering, beads, or charms. As well as the brooch, I have added a variety of extra buttons and fabric trimmings to the jacket.

*See page 116 for the fabric brooch instructions.*

*crafty ways to*
*customize your coat*

# bags of all shapes and sizes

I'm of the opinion that you can never have too many bags, hence this choice of three different styles.

The bucket bag shown on the left has a great slouchy shape and has been lined in a contrasting fabric, both for interest and for strength. You could use an even stronger lining fabric—canvas, for instance—but I like the softness of ordinary cotton.

The simple shopper bag (above left) is a really useful design, as you can size the pattern up or down or change the shape completely. This bag takes very little fabric and is a lovely way to use up small pieces. Experiment with different fabrics front and back, make contrasting handles, or pin on brooches, keyrings, or flowers.

Although a little more complicated than the shopper, the white shoulder bag (above right) is incredibly useful, especially in the summer months when a leather handbag looks too heavy with lightweight clothes. I have used coarse linen for this bag and have lined it with a pretty floral print.

*See pages 119, 120, and 122 for bag instructions.*

# *the perfect solution for*
# *wayward hair*

## hair tie

Even as a child, I could never understand how anyone could manage without a hair bow to keep wayward strands of hair out of their eyes. I still ponder this and am always to be found with something tied around my head, though it is more likely to be a piece of torn-off hem, or a fabric remainder too pretty to throw away. This head tie, however, is the perfect solution to my perennial problem. I must thank my mother for this—I have asked her to make me so many.

*See page 117 for the hair tie instructions.*

# child's patch skirt

This is the simplest way to make a skirt of any size, and you don't even need a paper pattern! The elastic waist allows room for growth and you can easily scale the skirt up or down in size—you could even make an adult version if you wish. The pockets can be made from the same material as the skirt, but I think it looks more effective to use a contrasting fabric. Make the pockets large enough to hold a child's favorite soft toy.

*the easiest-to-sew skirt ever*

This skirt has been made in soft cotton for summertime wear, but it would work just as well in a warmer fabric for the winter. Choose fabric that isn't too stiff—a soft fleece in bright colors would be ideal for young girls.

*See page 118 for skirt instructions.*

59

# lined wicker basket

The bonus of lining a wicker shopping basket is that when it inevitably begins to wear out at the base, you are less likely to lose precious tiny items which have found their way to the bottom of your basket. I tend to buy a new basket every year, and by the end of the season it has become rather less reliable.

Here I have lined an ordinary French shopping basket, as this is what I use as a handbag during the summer. The lining can easily be removed and inserted into a new basket. Informal striped, checked, or floral fabrics look particularly good against the wicker.

*See page 126 for the lining instructions.*

See page 126 for the lining instructions.

> ### lining a laundry basket
> You could adapt this idea to make a fabric lining for a wicker or plastic laundry basket, which will prevent delicate clothing snagging on the rough edges of the wicker, and improve the look of the plastic version.

# the perfect potting shed accessory

## lined seed basket

You cannot own enough baskets in my opinion, and a collection of old wire baskets is always very practical in the potting shed. For seeds, which need to be organized by date of planting, it is useful to have a lined basket for the inevitable seed spillage or pencil slipping through the holes.

Of course, a beautifully lined basket has a multitude of uses as well as being the starting point for a gift basket. Fill it with seed packets, a reel of gardener's twine, a trowel, and a packet of plant labels, wrap it up in cellophane or tissue paper, and you have the perfect gift for the passionate gardener. You can also adapt this project and make lined baskets to house cosmetics on the dressing table, correspondence on the desk, or keys on the hall table.

*See page 127 for seed basket instructions.*

# garden tool apron

At the first hint of spring I rediscover the potting shed and the renewed excitement of planting and planning for the summer. However, the potting shed always seems rather untidy and unkempt from the hasty dumping of pots and unplanted seeds at the end of autumn, when the gloom of the impending winter means my enthusiasm for gardening comes to an abrupt end.

The garden tool apron was one of the first things I made when embarking on this book, and I cannot remember feeling so very proud for such a long time. Using nothing more than an old scrap of canvas, this combined apron and tool holder is a terribly practical thing to own, or to give as a gift. The fact that it can be removed from around your waist and simply hung on the potting shed wall makes it all the more useful. It can be adapted to other hobbies or uses, such as a woodworking apron or a painter's apron.

*See page 124 for the garden tool apron instructions.*

*keep all those vital garden tools easily at hand with this apron*

gifts

# *the ideal present for a keen cook: a themed gift basket*

## gift baskets

These gift baskets are such a good idea for young and old alike, and can be themed for any occasion—holidays, birthdays, anniversaries. The baking tin forms the "basket" and it is filled with all the ingredients you need to make a batch of cookies, a loaf of bread, or a cake.

Simple fabric bags contain the measured dry ingredients (weigh them into plastic bags, secure the top, and pop them inside the fabric bags). The recipient just needs to add the wet ingredients. Other elements, such as shaped cookie cutters, a miniature rolling pin, wooden spoons or whisks, even a tiny bottle of brandy for a fruit cake, can be added.

The recipe can be hand written or printed from the computer, but I think that hand writing makes the gift more personal.

---

### to make the fabric bags

Cut two rectangles of fabric large enough to contain the ingredients. Stitch the two pieces of fabric together around three sides and sew a double-turned hem around the top open edge. Insert your ingredients and tie the bag closed with a strip of contrasting fabric or string. If you have made your bag from plain fabric, decorate it by stenciling on the words "cake" or "cookie mix" according to your recipe.

# *afternoon tea is the perfect excuse to take a break*

## placemat and napkin

I have only just realized what a difference a placemat can make! There is something very homely about making the effort to lay a tray prettily, and the extreme beauty of a single flower set on a tray can make such a difference. A scented blue hyacinth on a blue checked placemat for a sick friend, a pure white rose on white linen, a single peony on a birthday breakfast tray—all worth the pleasure they will bring. Make several of these placemats in different fabrics chosen to coordinate with your favorite china. You could even use this as the perfect excuse to buy odds and ends of china—all you need is one place setting.

Here I have used contrasting fabric for the back and the front of the placemat. When you have finished sewing the placemat, it is easy to make a matching napkin simply by cutting a large square of fabric and hemming it neatly on all four sides.

*See page 134 for the placemat instructions.*

*turn your afternoon pot of tea into something special by setting a pretty tea tray*

# cutlery roll

This is such a handy thing to have at-the-ready in the picnic basket. I always used to forget to pack essential things for picnics until I learned that by far the easiest way to avoid this is to have the picnic basket packed and ready to go with only the food to remember. As well as cutlery (which is very neat and nifty in this tie-up roll), I leave salt, pepper, a carving knife, napkins, picnic glasses, plates, a corkscrew, and rubbish bags stored in the picnic hamper. This means that when the sun shines unexpectedly on the weekend, I can just add picnic food and be on my way.

I made this cutlery roll out of a pretty checked dish towel—by this stage in the book you will have realized that, as always, it's anything for an easy life! A towel comes ready hemmed and is the perfect size for this project. However, if you wished, you could make one from fabric with napkins to match.

*See page 128 for the cutlery roll instructions.*

*perfect for summertime picnics*

# fabric-covered box files

There was a time when pretty box files were easy to get hold of. I remember my joy at buying some terribly expensive boxes from an interior design shop—they were an extravagance but they made such a difference to the shelves in my office, not to mention that terribly elusive thing in my life—organization.

The beauty of covering box files yourself is that you can co-ordinate them with the decor of the room or office, and turn an everyday object into something worthy of display. I have covered these files with vintage fabric, but any cotton fabric of a reasonable weight will work well.

*See page 132 for box file instructions.*

**matching accessories**

Why not make a matching set of stylish desk accessories by covering blotters, and ring binders with the same fabric?

# *a personal gift from you*

## buttoned pillows

I seem to have inherited a great many monogrammed napkins and have been searching for a good use for them. I think I've found the answer with this elegant pillow cover. I often find monogrammed napkins featuring friends' initials and if there are only one or two available, a pillow seems a more substantial and personal gift than a pair of old napkins!

The fact that the napkins are already hemmed means this project takes no more than half an hour to create, making it all the more pleasurable. An oblong cushion makes a change from the normal square shape, and the neat button fastening on the back is much quicker to stitch than inserting a zipper.

*See page 88 for the buttoned pillow instructions.*

### vintage fabrics

This pillow cover can easily be made using other vintage fabrics—remainders from worn linen sheets or pillowcases would work equally well. Placemats, which can often be bought inexpensively from antique shops and at yard sales, would also be ideal.

## lavender-filled heart

Lavender hearts are a very simple way to use up the tiniest piece of fabric, whether vintage or new. You can use two different fabrics, or the same fabric for back and front. Here a heart has been made to match a pillow cover, instantly turning an everyday cushion into a special scented pillow.

There is a multitude of things you can do with lavender-filled hearts: sew tiny ones onto greeting cards, or suspend them with ribbon loops from clothes hangers. Use flat, unfilled hearts for patching pillows, clothes, or bedspreads. Make them from red felt or ornate embroidered fabrics and use as holiday decorations, or string them together for a garland. Embroider initials on a silk heart to welcome a new baby into the world—the possibilities are endless!

*See page 89 for heart instructions.*

*embroider initials
on a silk heart
to welcome a new
baby into the world*

# fabric-covered coat hangers

There is nothing more pleasing than to have a complete set of matching hangers. It instantly makes your wardrobe appear more organized. Although sheer luxury would be a complete set of padded hangers, it is rare that one would ever buy enough to accommodate new clothes over the years and rarer still to find the same type a year after the first purchase! So these two projects show how to take control of your wardrobe cheaply, satisfyingly, and beautifully. One clothes hanger is given its own fabric sleeve, and the other is a simple wire hanger (the type often provided by dry cleaners) which has been given the five-star treatment.

The fabric sleeve is a pretty way to feminize those sturdy wooden hangers and to soften their appearance. This is a good way to use up sheets (either cotton or linen) that have seen better days, or any fabric remainders. The buttons or bows will prevent skirt loops from slipping off. For wooden hangers designed for hanging trousers, this is a neat way of disguising the ugly clip.

*See page 135 for instructions for making the coat hanger sleeve.*

---

### to cover the wire hanger

First make snips in the selvedge of some cotton fabric approximately ½in. (1.25cm) apart and tear off three strips. Start to wind the fabric around a wire clothes hanger starting at the hook. When you reach the end of the fabric strip, tie the next piece securely to the last. You can either leave the join exposed with a neat knot or wind the fabric over the join to hide it. Continue until the entire hanger is covered and end with a knot.

# *not just for children,*
## *this rabbit will appeal to all*

## rabbit doll

This darling creature is a copy of an ancient doll given to my son by his Australian godmother. The rabbit still hangs on a bedroom wall with her mate, who is dressed in dungarees, a work shirt, and straw hat. She makes an enchanting present, even more so if you are clever enough to equip her with a wardrobe of clothes. When my daughter, Kate, was young, my dream was to make her a doll with a wardrobe which was an exact replica of her own clothes—a school uniform, a bridesmaid dress, her ballet clothes.

As a child, I remember my mother making the most beautiful coat for one of my dolls. Years later, a similar coat was included in one of our Cabbages & Roses collections.

*See page 129 for the rabbit instructions.*

# *a neatly arranged desk top will instantly make you appear more organized*

## pencil cups

If, like me, you suffer from "washing machine blindness," you will have experienced the loss of beloved clothes by shrinking, fading, or dyeing entire laundry loads pink. I have still not found the answer to why it is always those things that you love most that are corrupted so irretrievably. I once owned a beautiful handknitted Fair Isle sweater for just two weeks before it was transformed by accidentally felting it in the washing machine. My normal procedure for these heartbreaking occasions is to leave the sad subject in the laundry until I cannot walk past it any longer, and then throw it away.

That's why I'm so excited to have found a solution (or, at least, a use) for felted wool (or felt, as it has now become). I am sure you will come up with a million more uses for stiff felt, but I thought these pencil cups were so simple and useful, and certainly a good way to use and remember treasured objects.

*See page 136 for pencil cup instructions.*

*the ritual of hanging a stocking by the fire adds to the holiday excitement*

## holiday stockings

These stockings have been made from antique quilts. They seemed such a good way of using quilts that have started to disintegrate and are beyond repair. Of course you can use many other fabrics, such as felt, brocade, velvet, or gingham. You can scale the stocking up or down in size using the template provided on page 141.

### to make the stocking

Enlarge the stocking template to your chosen size. Cut out a pair of stockings from antique quilted fabric and a hanging strap 2¾ x 21 in. (7 x 53cm). Stitch the two stocking pieces together, leaving the top straight edges open. Fold over the top edge 2¼ in. (6cm) to the wrong side and stitch in place. To make up the hanging strap, fold it in half and stitch the raw ends firmly to the inside of top hem. Your stocking is now ready to hang and fill with presents.

instructions

# tied tablecloth

### *you will need*

Cotton fabric

Sewing machine

3½ yds. (3.20m) of ½-in. (12-mm) wide ribbon

Needle and thread

Scissors

Tape measure

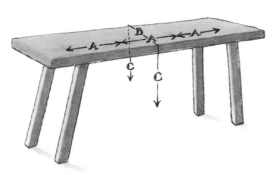

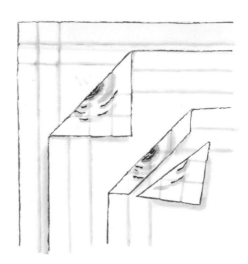

*1* Measure the length of your tabletop and decide how wide your three finished pieces of tablecloth need to be (A). Measure the width of the table (B) and the depth of the overhang required (C). Cut out three pieces of fabric to the width of the table (B) plus twice the overhang (C), times the calculated width of the tablecloths (A), adding a ¾in. (2cm) hem all around each piece for hems.

*2* To miter the corners, press over a double ⅜in. (1cm) hem along each side of one fabric piece and open out flat again. Matching up the press lines, turn over the corner of the fabric so that a diagonal fold passes through the point where the two inner press lines cross. Press the diagonal fold in place and then trim away the pointed corner, leaving a ⅜in. (1cm) hem.

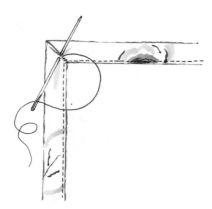

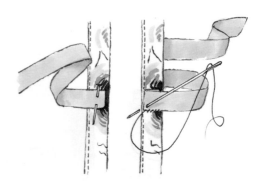

*3* Re-fold the hems and pin the diagonal mitered edges in place. Machine stitch the hems in place and then slipstitch the mitered corner edges together. Repeat steps 2 and 3 with remaining tablecloths.

*4* Lay the cloths over the table, making sure that the overhangs are level at each side of the table. Mark the positions where each set of ties will be fixed with pins. Pin each set of ribbon ties in place, making sure each tie matches up accurately with its opposing number, and stitch firmly in place. Neaten ribbon ends by trimming them diagonally.

# monogrammed pillow

### *you will need*

A rectangular piece of antique linen fabric two and a half times the width of your pillow, by the depth of your pillow, plus 1¼in. (3cm) for seam allowances

Square pillow form

Felt square

Traced, or computer-printed, initial or lettering

Tape measure

Scissors

Sewing machine

Needle and thread

Pins

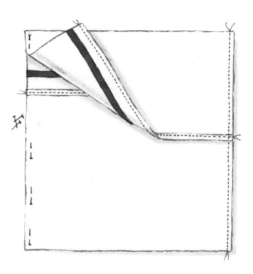

*1* Turn over a ⅜in. (1cm) double hem down both short ends of the fabric and stitch in place.

*2* With right sides facing, fold the fabric across its width into a square shape to fit the size of your pillow form, overlapping the hemmed ends at the center. Pin and machine stitch the sides together. Turn the cover right side out and press.

*3* Using your traced or printed lettering as a template, cut out the letters from the felt and arrange on to the front cover. Pin in place. Hand-sew the lettering to the cover, making sure you don't catch the back cover with the stitching as you sew. Insert the pillow form through the back opening.

*4* If you need to launder your cover frequently, it may be best to make your lettering detachable, as some felt is not colorfast when laundered. The best way to do this is use small pieces of Velcro tape hand-sewn to the front of the cover, to fasten the letters in place.

# drawn thread napkin ring

### *you will need*

A piece of even-weave linen 9¼ x 4¾ in. (23.5 x 12cm)

Needle and thread

¼ in. (6mm) diameter pearl button

Fine pointed scissors

Tape measure

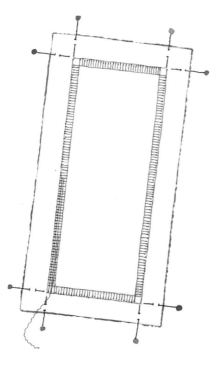

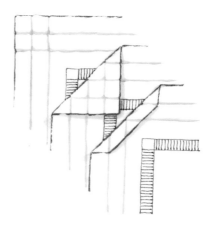

*1* Measure the hem depth 1½ in. (4cm) all around the linen piece and mark with pins. Start to withdraw threads up to a depth of ¼ in. (6mm) inside the hemline. Do not withdraw threads right across the fabric, but only those to form a rectangle inside the hem allowance. To do this, carefully cut the threads at the center and withdraw them gradually from each side edge to within the hem measurement.

*2* Turn back and press a double-turned ½ in. (1.25cm) hem up to the edge of the drawn threads. To miter the corners, open out the hems flat again. Matching up the press lines, turn over one corner of the fabric so that a diagonal fold passes through the point where the two inner press lines cross. Press the diagonal fold in place and then trim away the pointed corner, leaving a ⅜ in. (1cm) hem. Repeat on the remaining corners.

*3* Refold the hems and baste in place. Thread your needle and bring the working thread out two threads down from the space of the drawn threads, through the folded hem edge at the right-hand corner. Pass the needle behind four loose threads and bring the needle out to the front.

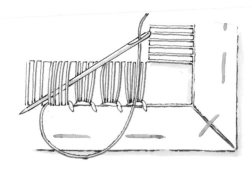

4 Move the needle back to the right and pass it back under the same four threads, consequently wrapping the thread around the loose threads. Bring the needle back out two threads down through hem fold in readiness for the next stitch. Continue all around the hem edge of the drawn threads, catching the hem in place at the same time.

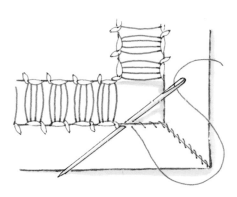

5 Repeat steps 3 and 4 on the inner edge of the drawn threads to complete the drawn thread work. Remove the basting threads.

6 Slipstitch the edges of the miters together and the square edges of the drawn thread corners.

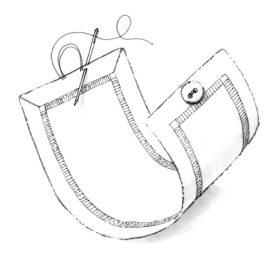

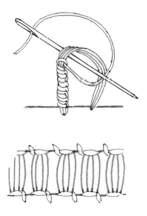

7 Stitch the button centrally to the hem at one short end of the strip and form a button-loop to correspond at the opposite end. To do this, make four looped stitches ¼ in. (6mm) apart, making sure that your button will pass through the loop.

8 To complete the button-loop, work buttonhole stitch closely around the looped stitches, keeping the looped edge of the buttonhole stitch to the inside.

# buttoned pillows

## *you will need*

Vintage monogrammed linen sheet, or damask tablecloth

Rectangular pillow form

Tape measure

Scissors

Sewing machine

Needle and thread

Two ⅝ in. (15mm) buttons

Tailor's chalk

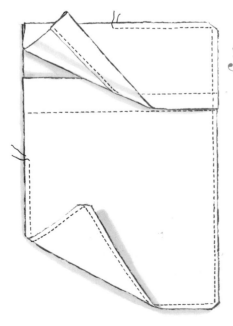

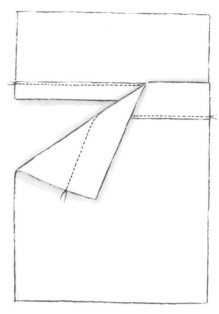

*1* Measure the length and width of your pillow form. Cut out a front cover to these measurements, centralizing the monogram and adding a ⅝ in. (1.5cm) seam allowance all around. Cut out one back cover to the same size as the front and a smaller back piece the width of the pillow form, by 8½ in. (21.5cm), adding a ⅝ in. (1.5cm) seam allowance all around.

*2* On one long edge of the small back piece, turn over a ⅝ in. (1.5cm) hem to the right side and press in place. Fold over a further 1½ in. (4cm) hem, press, and machine stitch in place. Repeat on one short edge of the large back piece, pressing over a 1½ in. (4cm) hem and then a further 2¼ in. (6cm) hem. Stitch in place.

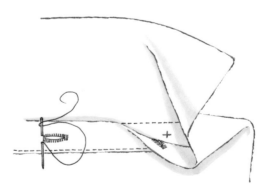

*3* Lay the front cover face up on a flat surface and place the large back piece face down on top, with raw edges level. Place the smaller back on top, overlapping the hemmed edges and keeping raw edges level. Sew the pieces together around all sides, taking a ⅝ in. (1.5cm) seam. Trim diagonally across seam turnings at each corner and turn the cover right side out.

*4* Using tailor's chalk, lightly mark the position of two vertical buttonholes centrally along the larger back's hem, spacing them evenly apart. Cut slits along the marked lines. Work buttonhole or blanket stitch along both edges, finishing with a few straight stitches to secure. Mark the position of the buttons, through the buttonholes, on the smaller back's hemmed edge and stitch the buttons place.

# lavender-filled heart

### *you will need*

Vintage cotton or linen fabric to match your pillow cover

Needle and thread

Dried lavender or fine pot pourri

A button

Brown paper for a template

Pencil and scissors

Pinking shears

Safety pin (optional)

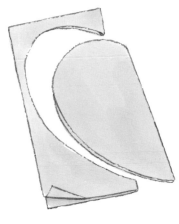

*1* Fold the brown paper in half and draw one half of a heart shape along the folded edge, to your desired size. Cut out the shape through both layers of paper. Open the template out flat and use to cut out two heart shapes from fabric using pinking shears.

*2* With wrong sides facing, stitch the two fabric pieces together around the edges, taking a ¼ in. (6mm) seam and leaving an opening on one side.

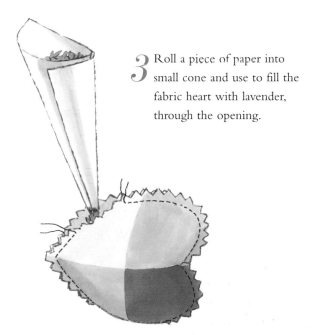

*3* Roll a piece of paper into small cone and use to fill the fabric heart with lavender, through the opening.

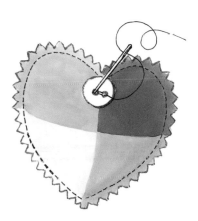

*4* Stitch the opening closed and sew a button to the top to decorate. Fasten the heart to the front of the pillow using either a safety pin or a few small stitches.

# linen easy-sew curtain

### *you will need*

Antique linen sheet

Pincer clip curtain rings

Curtain pole

Pins

*1* Measure the depth of your window from the pole to the floor. Fold the top edge of the sheet over to create a valance to your desired length. Remember to allow for extra length in your measurements if you want the curtain to "puddle" on the floor.

*2* With the top edge of the sheet still folded over, fold the sheet in half lengthways to determine the central point and mark the position along the top folded edge with a pin.

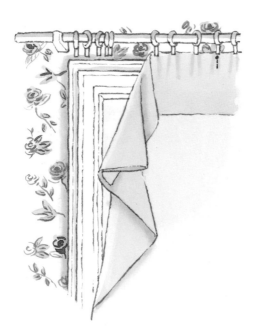

*3* To hang the curtain, start by clipping the middle curtain ring to the central position marked with the pin. Clip the remaining rings to the top folded edge, spacing them evenly along the length.

# café curtains

### *you will need*

Dish towels

Sewing machine

Needle and thread

Tape measure

Café rod and rings

*1* Measure the length and width of your window, making sure that the dish towels will be long enough to reach the windowsill. The number of dish towels will depend on the fullness you require; usually this is one and a half times the width of your window. Remember to launder your dish towels before you begin to allow for any shrinkage.

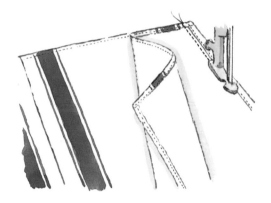

*2* With right sides facing, pin the dish towels together along their long edges. Using a zipper foot on your sewing machine, stitch the dish towels together to form a single curtain, sewing as close to the dish towel hems as possible. Press seams open.

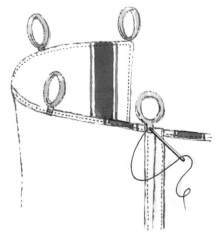

*3* Stitch the curtain rings to the dish towel curtain, spacing them at equal intervals along the top hemmed edge.

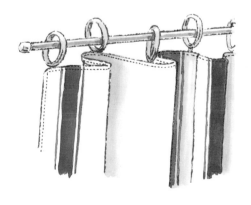

*4* Thread the rings on to the café rod and fix in place on the window frame.

# lampshade cover

## *you will need*

Cotton fabric
Gathered curtain heading tape 1 in. (2.5cm) wide
Sewing machine
Needle and thread
Plain lampshade

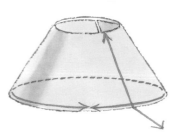

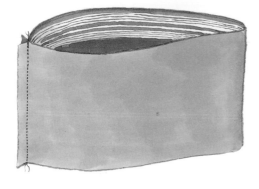

*1* Measure the depth of the lampshade and around the base circumference. Add 6 in. (15cm) to the depth measurement for hems and multiply the circumference measurement by one and a half. Cut out a piece of fabric to these measurements.

*2* Fold the fabric in half, right sides facing, and taking a ⅝ in. (1.5cm) seam machine stitch the short edges to form a fabric ring. Neaten the edges if desired.

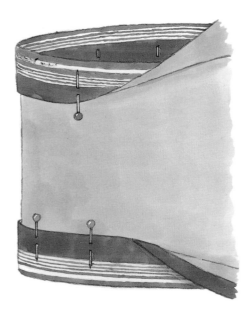

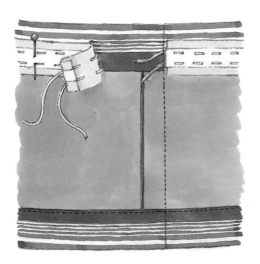

*3* Along the lower edge of the ring, fold over ⅜ in. (1cm) and then another 1½ in. (4cm) to form the base hem. Press in place and then machine stitch close to the first folded edge. Along the top edge of the fabric, fold over 1½ in. (4cm) hem and press.

*4* Starting and finishing at the side seam, pin the curtain heading tape to the top hem, overlapping the top edge of the tape by ⅜ in. (1cm) covering the raw edge of the hem. Machine stitch the tape in place along the top and bottom edges. Pull up the tape draw-cords to gather to fit the top of your lampshade. Secure the cords. Place on top of the lampshade.

# contrasting tie-top curtains

### you will need

Printed cotton fabric

Contrast printed fabric

Matching ribbon ⅜ in. (1cm) wide

Tape measure

Scissors

Sewing machine

Matching thread

Pins

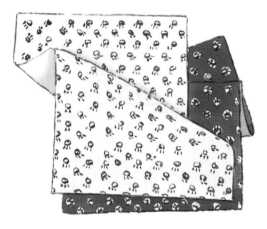

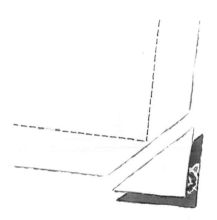

*1* To work out how much fabric you will need, measure from the base of your curtain pole to your desired length, adding 1½ in. (4cm) for hems, and from one side of the door/window to the other, multiplying this measurement by one and a half times. Cut out one main piece of fabric and one contrast piece of fabric for each curtain.

*2* Place the two pieces of fabric right sides together and stitch around three sides, taking a ⅝ in. (1.5cm) seam. Trim diagonally across the seam turnings at each corner to reduce the bulk.

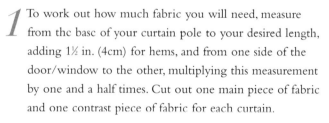

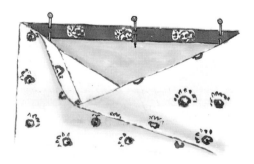

*3* Turn the curtain right sides out and press the seamed edges flat. Press a 1 in. (2.5cm) hem to the wrong side along the top raw edges and mark the positions of the ties along one top edge with pins, spacing them roughly 6 in. (15cm) apart.

*4* Cut the correct number of ribbon ties, each 20 in. (51cm) long. Fold each ribbon piece in half and pin the folded end to the top edge at the tie positions. Machine stitch the top pressed hem edges together, sandwiching the ribbon ties in-between.

# muslin canopy

### *you will need*

Printed cotton voile

Top template (see page 137)

26 in. (66cm) diameter hoop

3½ yds. (3.2m) of ⅜ in. (1cm) wide white cotton tape

1 in. (2.5cm) wide white bias binding

8 in. (20cm) of 1 in. (2.5cm) wide white cotton webbing

Sewing machine

Needle and matching thread

Tape measure

Pins

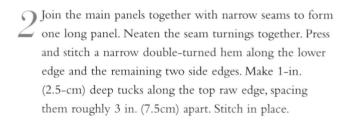

*1* Measure from the point that you want to hang your canopy to the floor and subtract 14 in. (35.5cm) from the measurement. Cut nine lengths of cotton voile to the calculated measurement and trim away the selvedge from the edges of each fabric piece. Enlarge the top template to full size and cut out eight pieces from fabric.

*2* Join the main panels together with narrow seams to form one long panel. Neaten the seam turnings together. Press and stitch a narrow double-turned hem along the lower edge and the remaining two side edges. Make 1-in. (2.5-cm) deep tucks along the top raw edge, spacing them roughly 3 in. (7.5cm) apart. Stitch in place.

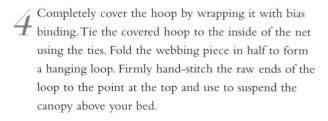

*3* Stitch the top sections together with narrow seams and neaten the turnings together. Cut the cotton tape into eight equal lengths. Fold each piece in half and pin the folded edge of each tape to the seams around the raw edge. With right sides facing, stitch the tucked top edge of the main panel to the lower edge of the top, stitching the ties in place at the same time and overlapping the main panel neatened side edges at the front.

*4* Completely cover the hoop by wrapping it with bias binding. Tie the covered hoop to the inside of the net using the ties. Fold the webbing piece in half to form a hanging loop. Firmly hand-stitch the raw ends of the loop to the point at the top and use to suspend the canopy above your bed.

# bedroom curtains

*you will need*

Fine printed cotton fabric
Sew-and-stick Velcro tape
Sewing machine
Needle and matching thread
Tape measure
Pins

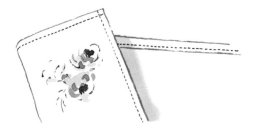

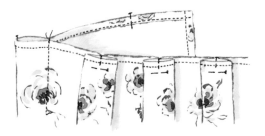

*1* To work out how much fabric you will need, measure from the top of the window frame to the floor, adding 2½ in. (6cm) for hems, and from one side of the window to the other, multiplying this measurement by two. Cut out the fabric to this measurement and neaten all edges with a double-turned ⅝ in. (1.5cm) hem.

*2* Mark the pleat positions along the top edge with pins, placing the first and last pin 4 in. (10cm) in from the side and spacing the others evenly between, approximately 8 in. (20cm) apart. Fold the fabric vertically, wrong sides together, at one pin position. Working 2 in. (5cm) in from the fold, machine stitch down for 4 in. (10cm) from the top edge, keeping parallel to the fold. Repeat at each pin position. Refold the pleats so that the pins lie on top of the seams. Pin in place.

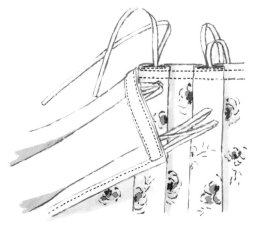

*3* For each pleat, cut a tie strip measuring 33 x 2 in. (84 x 5cm). With wrong sides together, press one tie strip in half along its length. Open the strip out flat and press the short ends ⅜ in. (1cm) to the wrong side, then press the long raw edges over to meet at the central press-line. Re-fold the strip with the raw edges inside and machine stitch the long pressed edges together. Repeat with remaining tie strips.

*4* Fold each tie in half and insert the folded end into the top of each pleat at the seams. Pin and machine stitch across the top of each pleat, sandwiching the ties in place and the pleats flat. Stitch the sew side of the Velcro tape to the top edge of the curtain and stick the hook side to the window frame. Tie the bows, and fix the curtain to the window using the Velcro tape.

# hot water bottle cover

### *you will need*

Printed cotton fabric

Contrast lining fabric

Paper for making template

Pencil

Scissors

Hot water bottle

Sewing machine

Needle and thread

Tape measure

Pins

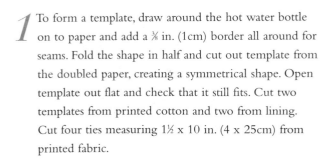

*1* To form a template, draw around the hot water bottle on to paper and add a ⅜ in. (1cm) border all around for seams. Fold the shape in half and cut out template from the doubled paper, creating a symmetrical shape. Open template out flat and check that it still fits. Cut two templates from printed cotton and two from lining. Cut four ties measuring 1½ x 10 in. (4 x 25cm) from printed fabric.

*2* With right sides facing, stitch the two printed fabric pieces together around the three straight sides, taking a ⅜ in. (1cm) seam and leaving the top shaped edges open. Repeat with the two lining pieces.

3 Clip into the curved seam turnings around the lower stitched edges and the top raw open edges of both covers. Carefully press the clipped top edges ⅜ in. (1cm) to the wrong side.

4 Turn the printed cover right side out and insert the lining inside, matching up the side seams and the top pressed edges. Pin the top edges together.

5 With wrong sides together, press the tie strips in half lengthways. Open the strips out flat and press long raw edges to the wrong side to meet down the center. Re-fold the strips with raw edges inside. Hand-whipstitch the pressed edges of the ties together.

6 Insert one end of each tie between the fabric layers at the neck of the cover. Make sure that the corresponding ties are level. Pin the ties in place.

7 Whipstitch the top pressed edges of the cover together. Stitch the ties in place at the same time, sandwiching them between the two layers of fabric.

# tied pillow cover

### *you will need*

One piece of contrast fabric the same size as your pillow form,
plus ⅝ in. (1.5cm) all around for seams

Two pieces of fabric measuring the length by two-thirds of the width of your pillow form,
plus ⅝ in. (1.5cm) all around for seams

Four strips of fabric 14 x 1½ in. (35.5 x 4cm)

Square pillow form

Tape measure

Sewing machine

Needle and thread

Pins

*1* Cut out the fabric following the measurements given in the "You will need" list. Fold over a ⅝ in. (1.5cm) hem down one long side of both narrower front fabric pieces and machine stitch in place.

*2* Fold over another 1½ in. (4cm) down each hemmed edge and press in place to form facings. Baste the raw facing ends in place.

*3* Machine topstitch down one facing edge close to the pressed edge. Trim this front piece down to measure half the width of your pillow, plus ⅝ in. (1.5cm) for a seam allowance.

4 Lay the contrast back piece face up on a flat surface and place the narrowest front face down on top, with the raw edges level. Place the wider front on top, overlapping the hemmed edges and keeping raw edges level. Sew the pieces together around all sides, taking a ⅝ in. (1.5cm) seam.

5 Trim diagonally across the seam turnings at corners to reduce the bulk. Turn the cover right side out and press.

6 With wrong sides together, press one tie strip in half along its length. Open the strip out flat and press the long raw edges over to the wrong side to meet at the central press-line. Re-fold the strip with the raw edges inside and machine stitch the long pressed edges together. Repeat with the remaining tie strips.

7 Lay the cover out flat and use pins to mark the edge of the overlap on the piece of fabric to form the lower part of the front overlap. Using more pins, mark the position of the ties on the front overlap to correspond on the pin line below, placing them roughly a quarter of the way in from the side edges of the cover.

8 Hand-stitch the ties to the hem of the front overlap and to the right side of the underlap to correspond. Insert the pillow form through the front opening and tie the bows to close the cover.

# bed skirt

### *you will need*

Checked cotton fabric

Sheeting fabric

Sewing machine

Matching thread

Tape measure

Pins

*1* Excluding the mattress, measure the length and width of your bed base and the height from the top to the floor. From checked fabric, cut the following skirt pieces: for the foot, cut one piece to width plus 20 in. (51cm) for pleats, by the height measurement, adding a ⅝ in. (1.5cm) seam to all sides. For the sides, cut two pieces the length plus 23 in. (58cm) for pleats, by the height measurement, adding a ⅝ in. (1.5cm) seam to all sides. From sheeting, cut one top piece to the length and width measurements, adding a ⅝ in. (1.5cm) seam allowance to all sides.

*2* With right sides facing, stitch the side skirts to each end of the foot skirt to form one long strip, taking a ⅝ in. (1.5cm) seam. Neaten the seam turnings together and press the seams flat.

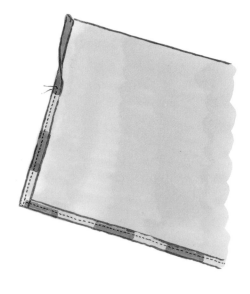

*3* Press a ¼ in. (6mm) hem to the wrong side along the lower edge and remaining two short ends of the skirt. Then press over a further ⅜ in. (1cm) hem and machine stitch the hems in place.

4 Fold the foot skirt in half and mark the central position with a pin on the raw edge. Measure 3 in. (7.5cm) in from each neatened end of the skirt and mark the positions with pins. Fold each side skirt in half, bringing the 3 in. (7.5cm) pins to meet the foot seams. Mark the central positions as before with a pin.

5 Measure along the top raw edge 5 in. (12.5cm) each side of the pins and mark these positions with more pins. To form inverted pleats, fold the fabric bringing the outer pins to meet at the central pin. Pin and baste the pleats in place.

6 Measure 5 in. (12.5cm) each side of the foot seams and mark positions with pins on the raw edge. Fold the last two pleats by bringing pins to meet at the seams. Pin and baste the pleats in place. You should now have five full pleats and a half pleat at each end, with 3 in. (7.5cm) of skirt extending beyond.

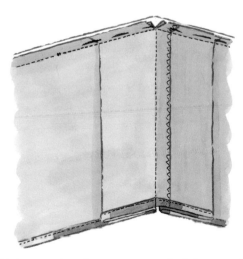

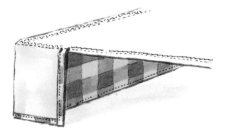

7 Fold the top piece into quarters to find the central positions of each side and mark with pins. With right sides facing, pin the skirt to the top, matching up the pleats to the central pins and corners. Snip into the skirt seam turnings at each corner to help it turn the corner. Sew the skirt in place, taking a ⅝ in. (1.5cm) seam. Neaten the seam turnings together.

8 Neaten the remaining raw edge of the top piece. Press the neatened edge ⅝ in. (1.5cm) to wrong side and stitch the hem in place. Slip the skirt over the bed base and place the mattress on top.

# chair slipcover

## *you will need*

Printed cotton fabric

Square pillow form

Thick piping cord, enough to go around edge of the pillow form

1¼ yds. (1.15m) of ⅜-in. (1-cm) of white cotton tape

Tape measure

Scissors

Sewing machine

Needle and thread

Two ⅝ in. (15mm) buttons

Tailor's chalk

*1* Measure the size of your pillow form. Cut out two square pieces from fabric to these measurements, adding a ⅝ in. (1.5cm) seam allowance all around. Cut out a smaller rectangular piece the size of the pillow form, by two-thirds the width, adding a ⅝ in. (1.5cm) seam allowance all around.

*2* Measure around the circumference of your piping cord and cut out a bias-grain fabric strip to this measurement, by the required length, adding a ⅝ in. (1.5cm) seam allowance to all sides. To cover the cord, place the piping cord down the center of the bias strip on the wrong side. Bring the long edges together around the cord and stitch down the length close to the cord, using a zipper foot on your machine.

*3* Place the piping on to the right side of one of the fabric squares, with cord facing inward and raw edges level. To help the piping go around the corners, snip into the seam turnings to help it bend. Baste the piping in place.

*4* To join the ends of the piping cord, unpick the machine stitches for about 2 in. (5cm) at each end and fold back the bias strip. Trim the two cord ends so they butt together, then bind the ends together with thread. Turn under ¼ in. (6mm) of fabric at one end of the bias strip to neaten, and slip this end over the raw opposite end. Baste ends neatly in place.

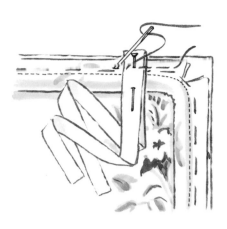

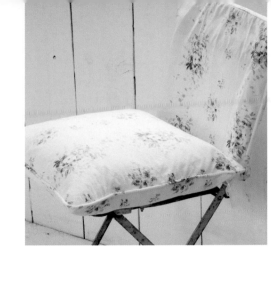

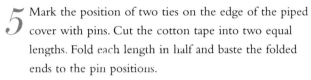

5 Mark the position of two ties on the edge of the piped cover with pins. Cut the cotton tape into two equal lengths. Fold each length in half and baste the folded ends to the pin positions.

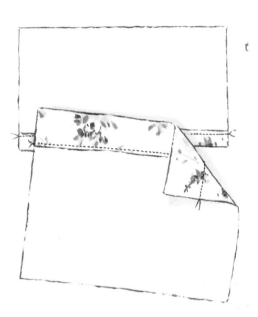

6 On the remaining fabric square, press over a double-turned 1¾ in. (4.5cm) hem along one side and stitch in place. On the rectangular piece, press over a double-turned ¾ in. (2cm) hem down one long edge and stitch in place.

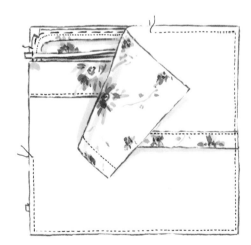

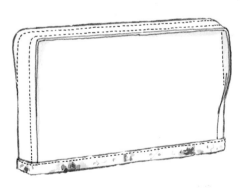

7 Lay the piped cover face up on a flat surface and place the larger hemmed piece face down on top, with raw edges level. Place the rectangular piece on top, overlapping the hemmed edges and keeping raw edges level. Pin, baste, and stitch the layers together close to the cord, using a zipper foot on your machine and sandwiching the ties in place at the same time. Turn cover right side out and make button fastenings for the back opening as shown in step 4 of the "Buttoned Linen Pillow" on page 88.

8 Measure the width and depth of your chair back. Cut two pieces of fabric to these measurements adding a ⅝ in. (1.5cm) seam all around. Cut a gusset 2 in. (5cm) wide by the width of the chair back plus twice the depth, adding 1¼ in. (3cm) to the length for seams. With right sides facing, stitch the gusset between the two fabric pieces. Turn cover right side out and press. Press a ¼ in. (6mm) hem to the wrong side along the lower edge, then a further ⅜ in. (1cm) and stitch in place.

# bolster pillow

### *you will need*

Printed cotton or linen fabric

Bolster pillow form

Brown paper for a template

Pencil

Scissors

Sewing machine

Needle and thread

Zipper

Two self-cover buttons

Tape measure

Pins

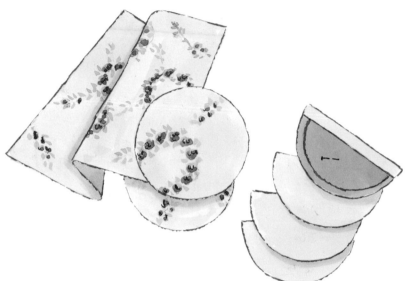

*1* Measure the length, circumference, and diameter of your bolster pillow form. For the end piece, draw a circle on paper to the diameter of the pillow form and add ⅝ in. (1.5cm) seam allowance all around.

*2* Cut a main fabric piece to the length of the pillow form by the circumference, adding a ⅝ in. (1.5cm) seam allowance to all sides. Using the template, cut out two end pieces from fabric. Fold the template in half and cut out four fabric pieces using the folded template, adding a ⅝ in. (1.5cm) seam allowance along the straight edge.

*3* With right sides together, fold the main fabric piece in half across its width, bringing the shorter edges together. Pin and baste the shorter edges together, taking a ⅝ in. (1.5cm) seam, to form a cylinder.

*4* Lay the zipper over the seam and mark the two ends of the zipper with pins. Remove the zipper and machine stitch the seam at each end, from the side edges to the pin markers. Press the seam open.

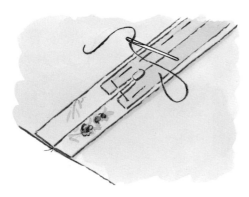

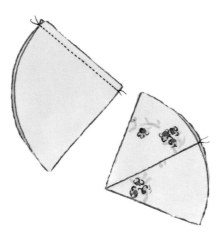

5 Lay the zipper face down onto the seam turnings, along the basted section, then pin and baste the zipper in place. Working from the right side and using a zipper foot on your machine, sew the zipper in place. Unpick the basting stitches and check that the zipper opens easily.

6 With right sides facing, fold one of the half-end pieces along its straight edge to form a triangular shape. Stitch down the straight edge, taking a ⅝ in. (1.5cm) seam allowance. Turn right side out and press flat with the seam running centrally down one side. Repeat with remaining half-end pieces.

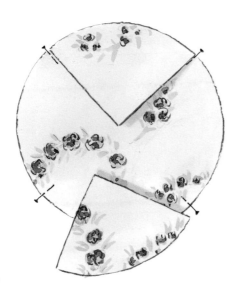

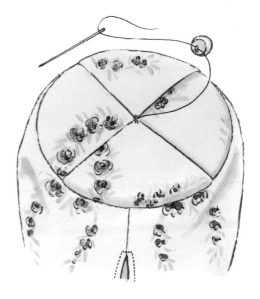

7 Fold an end piece into quarters and mark folds with pins on outer edge. Open out flat with right side uppermost. Place two triangular pieces opposite each other on top of the end between the pins, with raw edges level and seams facing down. Baste in place. Repeat with remaining end and triangles.

8 Undo the zipper and with right sides facing, pin and stitch the end pieces to the main piece, taking a ⅝ in. (1.5cm) seam. Turn the cover right side out. Hand-stitch the points of the triangular flaps to the center of each end and sew on a button to decorate. Insert the pillow form and close the zipper.

# envelope shoe bag

### *you will need*

Two pieces of printed toile de Jouy cotton fabric, approximately
22 × 11½ in. (56 × 29cm)

Two pieces of printed toile de Jouy cotton fabric, approximately
14 × 11½ in. (35.5 × 29cm)

Tailor's chalk

Ruler

Scissors

Sewing machine

Needle and thread

Fabric-covered button

Pins

Knitting needle (optional)

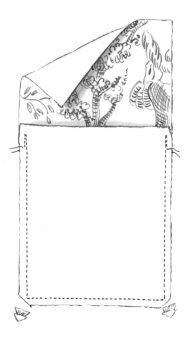

1 With right sides facing, place one small piece of fabric on top of one large piece, with both side edges and one short end level (the extending section will eventually form the flap). Stitch around the three level sides, taking a ⅝ in. (1.5cm) seam and starting and finishing the stitching ⅝ in. (1.5cm) down from the unsewn flap end. Trim diagonally across the seam turnings at each corner to reduce the bulk.

2 Fold the bag in half lengthways and mark the mid-point on the top edge of the flap with a pin. Open the bag out flat, and using the tailor's chalk and ruler, draw a diagonal line from each side edge to the pin position, as shown. Trim away the fabric along the lines to form a pointed flap. Repeat steps 1 and 2 with the remaining pieces of fabric to make the lining.

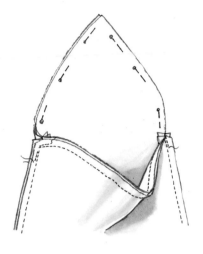

3 Turn the outer bag right side out and insert inside the lining, with the pointed flaps together and side seams matching. Pin the top edges of bag and lining together. Stitch along the straight front edge of the bag, taking a ⅝ in. (1.5cm) seam, starting and finishing at the side seam stitching.

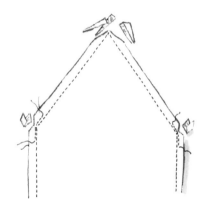

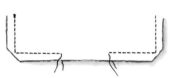

4 Stitch the pointed flaps together, taking a ⅝ in. (1.5cm) seam, starting and finishing at the side seam stitching. Trim diagonally across the seam turnings at the point and side seams to reduce the bulk.

5 Unpick approximately 2 in. (5cm) along the lining base seam and turn the bag right side out. Using a knitting needle or similar pointed object, carefully push out the corners and point in the flap.

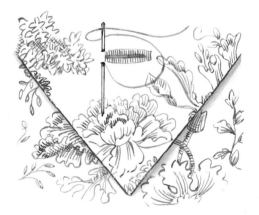

6 Slipstitch the unpicked lining seam edges together and push the lining down inside the bag. Press the seamed edges flat.

7 Mark the position of the buttonhole with tailor's chalk on the wrong side of the flap. Cut a slit along the marked line. Work buttonhole or blanket stitch along both edges, finishing with a few straight stitches to secure. Fold the flap down over the bag front and mark the position of the button through the buttonhole. Stitch the button to the bag front.

# drawstring jewelry case

### *you will need*

Two pieces of printed toile de Jouy cotton fabric, approximately 18 × 12 in. (45.5 × 30.5cm)

One strip of printed toile de Jouy cotton fabric, approximately 28 × 1½ in. (71 × 4cm)

Tape measure

Scissors

Sewing machine

Needle and thread

Large safety pin

Pins

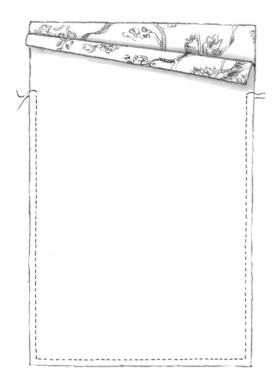

*1* Place the two pieces of same-size fabric right sides together and stitch around three sides, taking a ⅝ in. (1.5cm) seam, starting and finishing the stitching 4½ in. (11.5cm) down from the unsewn end.

*2* Press the side seams open and the top open edges ⅝ in (1.5cm) to the wrong side.

$3$ Press each top edge over a further 2 in. (5cm) to the wrong side. Machine stitch the top hems in place with two parallel rows of stitching, one close to the first pressed edge and the second 1 in. (2.5cm) above to form channels for the drawstring.

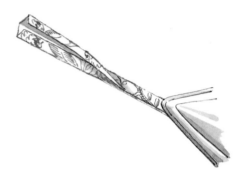

$4$ With wrong sides facing, press the fabric strip in half along its length. Open the strip out flat and press the long raw edges over to the wrong side to meet at the central press-line. Re-fold the strip with the raw edges inside and machine stitch the long pressed edges together to form the drawstring.

$5$ Using a safety pin, thread the drawstring through the lower stitched channels around the bag top hems, making sure the drawstring does not become twisted in the channel.

$6$ Unpick a few stitches from one end of the drawstring and overlap the open end over the opposite end. Sew ends together to form a loop.

$7$ Finally, slipstitch the open ends of the top hems together above the drawstring channels and pull on the drawstring to close the bag.

# zippered cosmetic case

### *you will need*

Printed cotton fabric

PVC lining fabric

14 in. (35cm) zipper

Template (see page 137)

Scissors

Sewing machine

Needle and thread

Tape measure

Pins

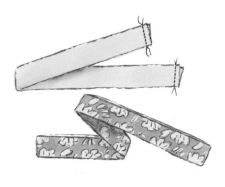

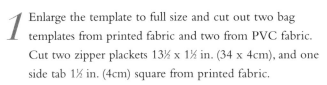

*1* Enlarge the template to full size and cut out two bag templates from printed fabric and two from PVC fabric. Cut two zipper plackets 13½ x 1½ in. (34 x 4cm), and one side tab 1½ in. (4cm) square from printed fabric.

*2* Fold the two zipper plackets in half lengthways, with right sides together, and stitch across the short ends, taking a ⅜ in. (1cm) seam. Turn to right side and press flat, keeping long raw edges level.

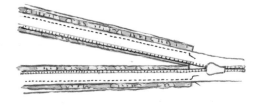

*3* Open the zipper and place it face down, with one tape lying on top of a placket. Position it centrally along the placket with the zipper teeth next to the long pressed edge. Sew the zipper in place, stitching close to the edge of the zipper tape. Repeat with remaining placket and other side of the zipper.

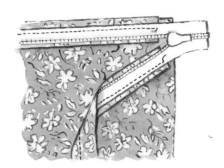

4 With right sides together, stitch the zipper plackets centrally to the top edge of the printed bag pieces, taking a ⅜ in. (1cm) seam and keeping the top raw edges level. Press the plackets upward so that they stand proud of the bag top.

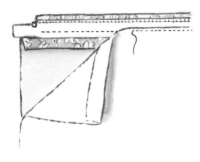

5 Fold over a ⅜ in. (1cm) hem along the top edge of one lining piece. With wrong sides together, place the lining on top of one bag side, keeping the raw side and base edges level and the folded top edge in-line with the zipper stitching. Stitch the lining to the bag along the folded edge, starting and finishing ⅜ in. (1cm) in from each side. Repeat with remaining lining and bag side.

6 Make up the side tab. With right sides together, stitch the bag side seams together, taking a ⅜ in. (1cm) seam and inserting the side tab into one seam as you sew (make sure you keep the bag lining out of the way as you sew). Stitch the bags together along the base, taking a ⅜ in. (1cm) seam. Press the seams open.

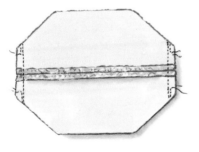

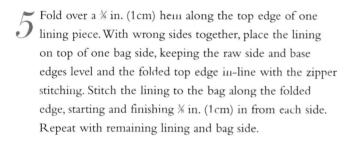

7 Re-fold the bag so that the base seam lies on top of one side seam and the raw open edges are level. Stitch the edges together, taking a ⅜ in. (1cm) seam. Re-fold bag, lining the base seam up with the other side seam and stitch remaining open edges together.

8 Close the zipper part way. With right sides facing, stitch the lining side seams together, starting at the base and sewing as close up to the zipper as possible. Stitch the lining along the base, leaving a large opening, and then continue following step 7. Turn the bag right side out and stitch the lining opening edges together.

# laundry bags

### *you will need*

Two pieces of printed cotton fabric, approx. 24 × 16 in. (61 × 41cm)

One strip of printed cotton fabric, approx. 15¼ × 2 in. (39 × 5cm)

Sewing machine

Matching thread

1 yd. (1m) cotton cord

Large safety pin

Pins

*1* Place the two pieces of fabric right sides together and stitch around three sides, taking a ⅜ in. (1cm) seam. Neaten seam turnings together if desired.

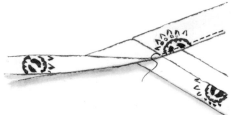

*2* Turn over and press a ⅜ in. (1cm) hem around the top open edges, then turn over a further 1 in. (2.5cm) hem and machine stitch in place.

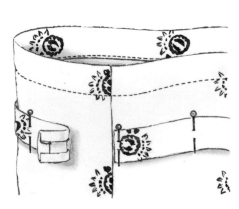

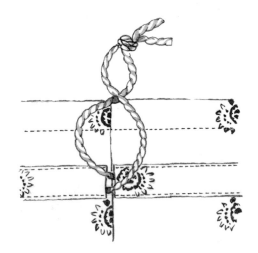

*3* Press a ⅜ in. (1cm) hem to the wrong side around all edges of the fabric strip. Starting about 2 in. (5cm) down from the top hemmed edge and at one side seam, pin the strip around the bag finishing back at the side seam. Stitch in place along both long edges of the strip, leaving the short ends open.

*4* Using a safety pin, thread the cord through the stitched channel around the top of the bag and knot the ends securely together.

# lavender pillow pocket

### *you will need*

Printed cotton fabric

A pillowcase

Scissors

Sewing machine

Needle and thread

Tape measure

Pins

Dried lavender

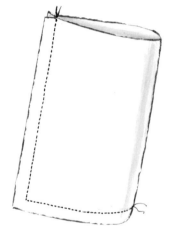

*1* Cut a rectangle from the printed fabric 9 x 7½ in. (23 x 19cm). With right sides facing, fold the rectangle in half, bringing the shorter edges together. Stitch the folded fabric together around two sides, taking a ⅜ in. (1cm) seam and leaving the top edge open.

*2* Turn the pocket right side out. Fold over a ¾ in. (2cm) hem to the wrong side around the top open edges. Press the hem in place and the pocket flat.

*3* Neatly slipstitch the top pressed edges of the pocket together.

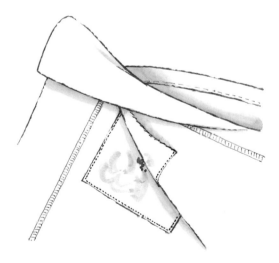

*4* Place the pocket on the front of the pillowcase close to one corner and next to the back flap opening. Pin the pocket in place through the top layer of fabric only, keeping the flap well out of the way. Stitch the pocket in place around three sides, leaving the slipstitched end open. Insert sprigs of lavender for a good night's sleep.

# kitchen apron

### *you will need*

Main printed cotton fabric

14 in. (35.5cm) square of contrast cotton fabric (or a matching tea towel)

Paper for scaling up templates on page 141

2¾ yd. (2.5m) of 1½-in. (4-cm) wide white cotton webbing

4 in. (10cm) of ¼-in. (6-mm) wide cotton tape

⅝ in. (15mm) button

Sewing machine

Needle and matching thread

Tape measure

Pins

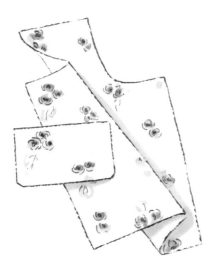

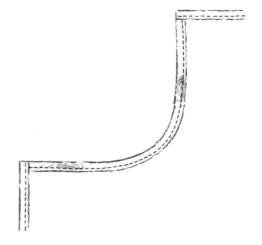

*1* Scale up the apron front and pocket patterns on to the large piece of paper, as indicated on page 141. Using the full-sized patterns, cut out one apron front and one pocket from the main fabric.

*2* Press over a double-turned ⅜ in. (1cm) hem to the wrong side around both curved edges of the apron front and stitch in place. Press over a double-turned ⅜ in. (1cm) hem to the wrong side along the remaining straight edges of the apron front and stitch in place.

*3* Press over a double-turned ⅜ in. (1cm) hem to the wrong side along the top edge of the pocket and stitch in place. Press a ⅜ in. (1cm) hem to the wrong side around the remaining edges of the pocket.

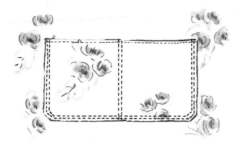

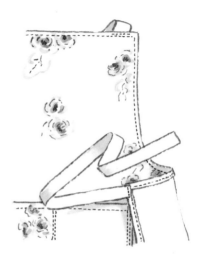

*4* With right sides up, lay the pocket centrally on to the apron with the base of the pocket lying parallel and 15½ in. (39cm) up from the apron's lower edge. Top stitch the pocket in place with two rows of stitching spaced ¼ in. (6mm) apart. Stitch vertically down the center of the pocket with two rows of stitching as before, to divide the pocket in two.

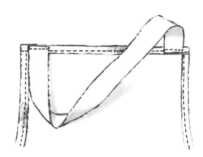

*5* Cut a 22½ in. (57cm) length of cotton webbing. Lay the apron wrong side up on a flat surface. Place one cut end of the webbing level with the top hemmed edge of the apron and ⅜ in. (1cm) in from one curved edge. Stitch it in place following the hem stitch-line. Fold webbing upwards so it extends above the apron and stitch across it again close to the top edge. Repeat with the other end of the webbing at opposite side to form neck loop.

*6* Cut the remaining webbing into two equal lengths for waist ties. Attach one end of each length to the side edges as shown in step 5 for the neck loop.

*7* Press over a double-turned ⅜ in. (1cm) hem to the wrong side along all edges of the contrast square and stitch in place (this isn't necessary if using a readymade tea towel). Fold the cotton tape in half and stitch the raw ends to one corner of the square, to form a hanging loop. Stitch the button to the corner of the pocket to hang the tea towel from.

*8* For the half apron, cut out the fabric following the half apron cutting line as shown on the pattern. Make up half apron as above, omitting references to the curved apron edges in step 2 and the neck loop in step 5.

# fabric brooch

## *you will need*

Large safety pin

Fabric scraps

Printed or embroidered nametag

Selection of sequins, flowers, and trimmings

Seed beads

Needle and thread

Beading needle

Glue

*1* Cut a rectangle of linen or cotton fabric approximately 2 x 4 in. (5 x 10cm). Appliqué the fabric with scraps of printed fabric, add a name tag; printed words will make the brooch look more interesting, so look out for sewn-in garment labels or cut out the words from down the selvedge of some printed fabric.

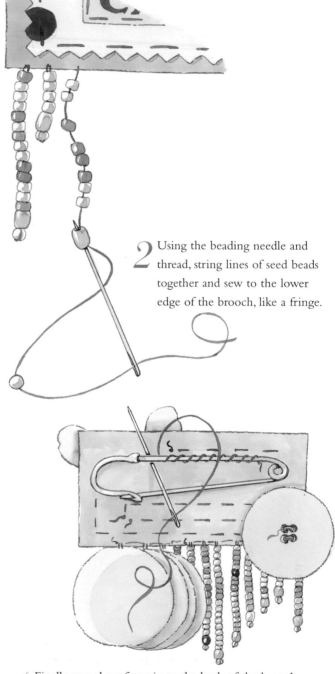

*2* Using the beading needle and thread, string lines of seed beads together and sew to the lower edge of the brooch, like a fringe.

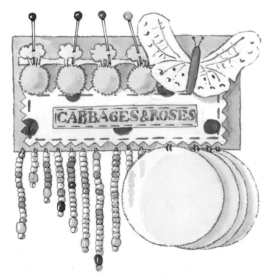

*3* Sew or glue on sequins, butterflies, or silk flowers, or make your own from felt. Add bobble or lace trims and buttons, until you feel happy with the effect.

*4* Finally, sew the safety pin to the back of the brooch, making sure that it is not visible from the right side. Pin to a jacket or sweater.

# hair tie

***you will need***

Paper for making a template
Pencil and ruler
Tape measure
Scissors
Printed cotton fabric
Sewing machine
Needle and thread
Pins

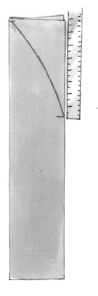

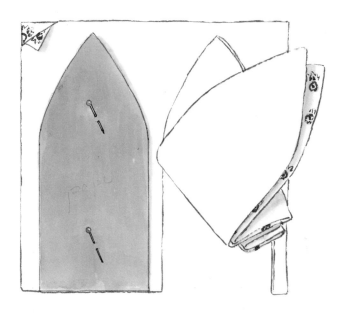

*1* Draw and cut out a rectangular strip of paper 19 x 8 in. (48 x 20cm). Fold the strip in half lengthways, bringing the long edges together. Measure 8 in. (20cm) down the long open sides from one short end and make a pencil mark. Draw a curved line from the pencil mark up to the fold on the same short end. Cut along the line through both layers of paper and open out flat for the template.

*2* Place the short straight edge of the template to the fold of fabric and cut out two hair tie pieces from the printed cotton.

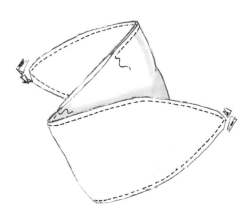

*3* With right sides facing, pin and machine stitch the two pieces of fabric together around the outer edges, taking a ⅜ in. (1cm) seam and leaving a 4 in. (10cm) opening along one straight side. Trim diagonally across the seam turnings at each point to reduce the bulk.

*4* Turn the hair tie right side out. Press the seamed edges flat and the opening edges ⅜ in. (1cm) to the wrong side. Slipstitch the opening edges closed. Then machine topstitch around all sides of the tie, working close to the edge.

# child's patch skirt

## *you will need*

Main printed cotton fabric

Contrast printed cotton fabric

Scissors

Sewing machine

Tape measure

Pins

22 in. (56cm) of 1-in. (2.5-cm) wide elastic

Large safety pin

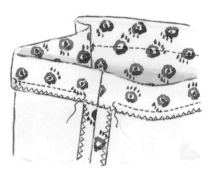

*1* Measure your child to obtain the finished skirt length (the dimensions given here are for a skirt to fit ages 2–6, but you can enlarge them if you wish). Cut a rectangle from main fabric 48-in. (122-cm) wide, by the required skirt length plus 4 in. (10cm) for hems. Cut out two pockets from the contrast fabric 10 x 7½ in. (25.5 x 19cm). With right sides facing, fold the main rectangle in half, bringing the shorter edges together. Stitch the two layers of fabric together down the side seam to form a circle, taking a ⅜ in. (1cm) seam. Neaten the seam turnings and press seam flat.

*2* Neaten the top and bottom edges of the circular skirt and press the hem edge 1 in. (2.5cm) to the wrong side. Machine stitch in place close to the neatened edge. Press the top edge 1½ in. (4cm) to the wrong side and sew in place, stitching 1¼ in. (3cm) down from the pressed edge and leaving a gap at the side seam. Using a large safety pin, thread the elastic through the top hem and adjust to fit. Stitch ends of elastic together and trim away surplus. Stitch the gap closed.

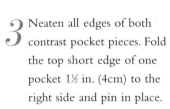

*3* Neaten all edges of both contrast pocket pieces. Fold the top short edge of one pocket 1½ in. (4cm) to the right side and pin in place. Machine-stitch down both short edges of the hem taking a ⅜ in. (1cm) seam. Turn the top hem right side out and press flat. Press remaining edges of pocket ⅜ in. (1cm) to the wrong side. Machine-stitch the top hem in place, stitching close to the neatened edge.

*4* Repeat with the remaining pocket. Try the skirt on your child and pin the pockets in position, making sure they are level. Machine-stitch the pockets in place around three sides, leaving the top hemmed edges open.

# shopper bag

## *you will need*

Two pieces of printed cotton, canvas, or linen fabric
approximately 17 x 15 in. (43 x 38cm)

Two strips of printed cotton, canvas, or linen fabric
approximately 27 x 3 in. (68.5 x 8cm)

Tape measure

Scissors

Sewing machine

Needle and thread

Pins

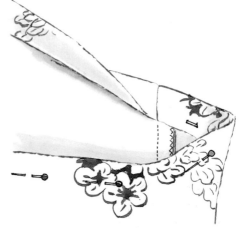

*1* Place the two-pieces of fabric right sides together and stitch around three sides, taking a ⅝ in. (1.5cm) seam and leaving the top edges un-sewn. Neaten turnings together and turn right side out.

*2* Fold over and press 1 in. (2.5cm) and then another 1 in. (2.5cm) to make a double hem along the top open edges. Pin in place.

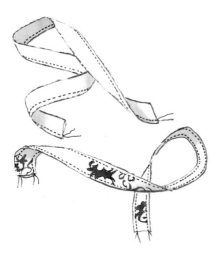

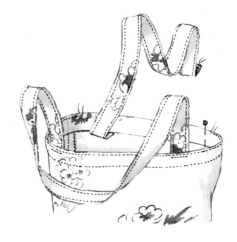

*3* To form the handles, fold each strip in half lengthways right sides facing, and stitch the long edges together with a ⅜ in. (1cm) seam. Turn strips right side out and press flat with the seams placed exactly along a pressed edge. Topstitch both long edges of the handles.

*4* Using pins, mark the handle positions on the bag's top hem, placing them 3 in. (7.5cm) in from the side seams. Press raw ends of handles ⅝ in. (1.5cm) to one side and slip ends under the loose hem edge. Pin in place. Machine stitch the hem around the top and bottom edges, anchoring the handles at the same time. Double-stitch over the handles to reinforce.

# pocket bag

## *you will need*

Canvas fabric for outer bag
Printed cotton fabric for lining
Bag templates on pages 139–139
Sewing machine
Matching thread
Scissors

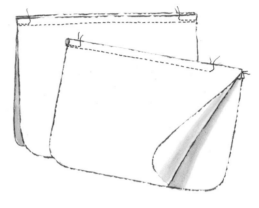

*1* Enlarge the bag templates to full size. From both the canvas and the printed fabric cut out two bag sides, two pockets, and two strap/gusset strips.

*2* With right sides facing, place the two canvas pocket pieces right sides together and stitch across the top straight edges, taking a ⅜ in. (1cm) seam. Press the seam open and then re-fold with wrong sides facing and stitch–line placed exactly on the folded edge. Press again and topstitch ¼ in. (6mm) in from the seamed edge.

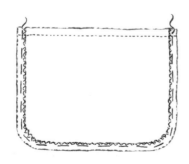

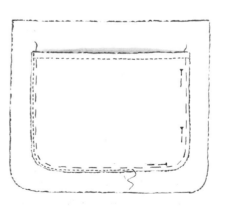

*3* Neaten the remaining raw pocket edges together and press ⅜ in. (1cm) to the wrong side. Baste the edges in place.

*4* Place the pocket centrally on to one canvas bag side, and with wrong side of pocket to right side of bag, pin, and machine stitch in place. Repeat steps 2, 3, and 4 with the lining pocket pieces and one lining bag side.

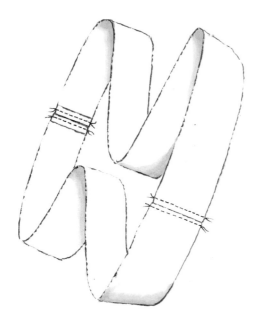

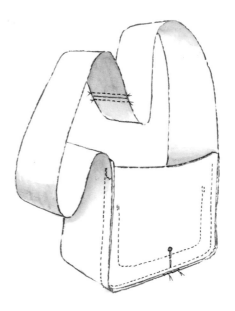

5 With right sides facing, stitch the canvas strap strips together at their short ends to form a ring, taking a ⅜ in. (1cm) seam. Press the seams open and topstitch the seam allowances, working ¼ in. (6mm) each side of the seams. Repeat with the lining strap/gusset strips. Make sure that both rings are the same size.

6 Fold each bag side in half and mark the central point along the base edge with a pin. With right sides facing, pin the canvas strap/gusset to one canvas bag side, matching the wider seam to the pin position. Machine stitch the gusset in place, taking a ⅜ in. (1cm) seam and starting and finishing ⅜ in. (1cm) from the top edge of the bag. Repeat with remaining canvas bag side and opposite side of the strip.

7 Press the raw top edges of the bag and each side edge of the strap ⅜ in. (1cm) to the wrong side, baste in place. Repeat steps 6 and 7 with the lining pieces.

8 With wrong sides facing, insert the lining into the canvas bag, making sure that the pockets are on opposite sides and that the straps and top edges are matching. Pin and machine stitch the bag and lining together along both sides of the strap and along the top edges, working close to the edge.

# bucket bag

### *you will need*

Printed linen for outer bag

Striped fabric for lining

Bag templates on page 140

Sewing machine

Needle and thread

Scissors

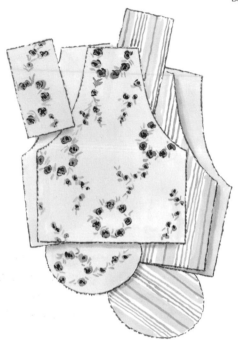

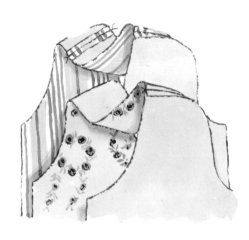

*1* Enlarge the bag templates to full size. From both printed linen and the striped lining fabric, cut out two bag sides, one base, and one strap.

*2* With right sides facing, stitch the short ends of the printed bag strap to the top edges of the printed bag sides. Repeat with the lining pieces.

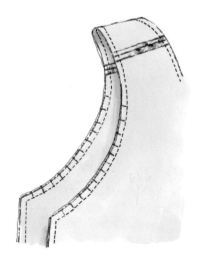

*3* With right sides facing, stitch the joined printed bag pieces to the joined lining pieces around the curved bag edges, taking a ⅝ in. (1.5cm) seam and keeping the strap seams level. Snip into the curves seam allowances and turn right side out. Press the seamed edges flat.

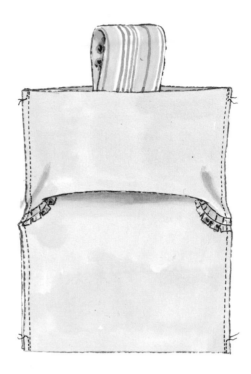

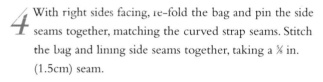

*4* With right sides facing, re-fold the bag and pin the side seams together, matching the curved strap seams. Stitch the bag and lining side seams together, taking a ⅝ in. (1.5cm) seam.

*5* Fold the printed bag base in half and mark the halfway positions at the edge with pins. Open out the base and, with right sides facing, stitch the base to the lower edge of the bag, matching the side seams to the pins and taking a ⅝ in. (1.5cm) seam.

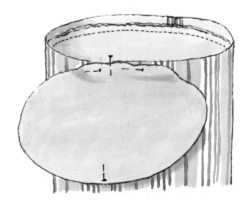

*6* Turn the printed bag right side out. Fold the lining base in half as before, and mark the halfway position with pins. With right sides facing, pin the lining base to the lower edge of the lining sides as far as you can, matching up the pins to the side seams. Stitch the base in place, taking a ⅝ in. (1.5cm) seam.

*7* Turn the lining right side out. Press opening edges ⅝ in. (1.5cm) to wrong side and slipstitch the opening edge closed. Push the lining down inside the bag to finish.

# garden tool apron

### *you will need*

Two pieces of striped cotton canvas fabric 26 × 10½ in. (66 × 27cm) for the apron

Two binding strips of cotton canvas 45 × 3 in. (114 × 7.5cm)

One strip of fabric 26 × 3 in. (66 × 7.5cm) for the tool strap

⅝ in. (15mm) diameter eyelets

Sewing machine

Matching thread

Tape measure

Pins

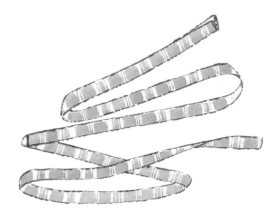

*1* Cut out the fabric following the measurements given in the list above. Place the two apron pieces right sides together and stitch down the two short sides and along one long side, taking a ⅝ in. (1.5cm) seam. Trim diagonally across the seam turnings at each corner to reduce the bulk. Turn right side out and press flat.

*2* Join the binding strips together at one short end to form one long strip. Press seam turnings open. Press the long edges of the binding ⅝ in. (1.5cm) to the wrong side, then press the strip in half lengthways with the raw edges inside.

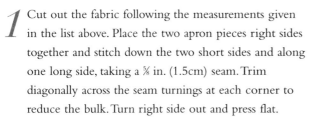

*3* Pin the binding over the top raw edges of the apron, placing the seam at the center and pin in place. Machine stitch the pressed edges of the binding together, sandwiching the apron in-between as you sew.

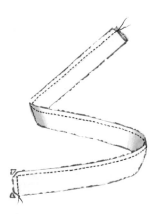

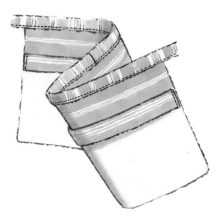

*4* Fold the strap strip in half lengthways with right sides together. Stitch across one short end and down one long side. Trim diagonally across the seam turnings at each corner to reduce the bulk. Turn right side out and press flat.

*5* Place the strap on the front of the apron 3⅓ in. (9cm) down and parallel to the top edge. Pin in place with the short neatened end level with one side edge and the raw end folded under, level with the opposite side edge. Machine-stitch in place down both ends.

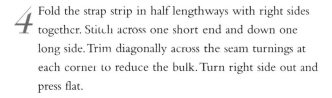

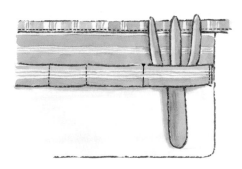

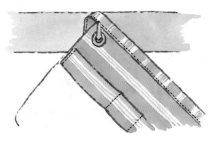

*6* Place your gardening tools under the strap and pin each side where you will need to stitch to hold them in place. Remove tools and vertically stitch down through the strap and apron at the positions marked.

*7* Finally, insert an eyelet into the top corners of the apron following the manufacturer's instructions. Use the eyelets to hang your tool apron up when not in use.

# lined wicker basket

### *you will need*

Cotton fabric

Wicker basket

Brown paper for making patterns

Pencil

Scissors

Sewing machine

Needle and matching thread

Tape measure

Pins

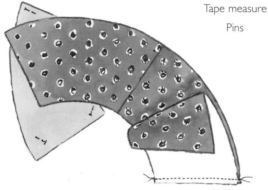

*1* Measure the depth and circumference of your basket and make a paper pattern, adding ⅝ in. (1.5cm) all around for seams and hems. Make a paper pattern for the base of the basket in the same way. Lay your paper patterns on the fabric and cut out the correct number of pieces. (You may need to join several pieces to get a piece large enough to fit around the circumference; if so, remember to allow extra for the seams.)

*2* Join the fabric pieces for the sides of the basket into a ring, taking ⅝ in. (1.5cm) seams. Press seams open. With right sides facing, pin the base piece to the lower edge of the ring, snipping into the seam turnings on the lower edge of the ring to help it fit around the curved edge. Stitch the pieces together, taking a ⅝ in. (1.5cm) seam.

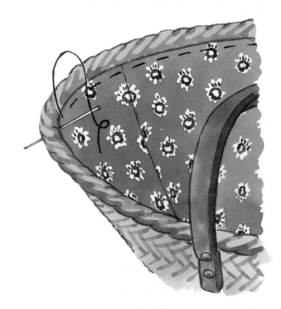

*3* Fold over and press a 1 in. (2.5cm) hem to the wrong side along the top raw edge.

*4* Insert the lining into the basket and pin the top edge in place. Hand-stitch the lining to the basket along the top pressed edge using running stitch.

# lined seed basket

## *you will need*

Cotton, canvas, or linen fabric

Wire basket or tray

Brown paper for a template

Pencil

Scissors

Sewing machine

Tape measure

Pins

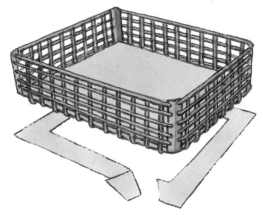

*1* Lay the wire basket or tray on brown paper and trace around the base. Fold the shape in half and cut out template from the doubled paper to create a symmetrical shape. Open the template out flat and check that it fits inside the basket base. Trim to fit if necessary. Cut out two base pieces from fabric, adding ⅝ in. (1.5cm) all around for seams.

*2* Measure the depth of the basket and add 2 in. (5cm) to the measurement for the fold-over top. Measure around the outer edge of the base template and then cut out two strips from fabric to these measurements, adding ⅝ in. (1.5cm) all around for seams.

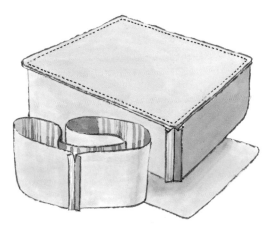

*3* With right sides facing, fold a side strip in half, bringing the short ends together. Stitch ends together to form a ring, taking a ⅝ in. (1.5cm) seam. Press the seam open and repeat with other strip. Stitch each side strip to a base panel, taking a ⅝ in. (1.5cm) seam and matching the side seam to one corner.

*4* Press the top raw edges of each piece ⅝ in. (1.5cm) to the wrong side. Turn one fabric piece right side out to form the lining and insert inside the other fabric piece, with wrong sides facing and corners and side seams matching. Pin and stitch the top pressed edges together. Insert into basket and fold over the top edge.

# cutlery roll

### *you will need*

A gingham tea towel

1¼ yds. (1.2m) of ¾-in. (2-cm) wide cotton tape

Sewing machine

Matching thread

Tape measure

Pins

*1* Fold over and pin a 5 in. (12.5cm) hem to the wrong side along one short end of the tea towel. Machine stitch the hem in place down both side edges and across the top.

*2* Fold the opposite short end 6 in. (15cm) to the wrong side and pin the hem in place. Cut the cotton tape in half and insert one end of each piece into the sides of the hem close to the top edge. Machine stitch the sides of the hem in place, sandwiching the ties in place at the same time.

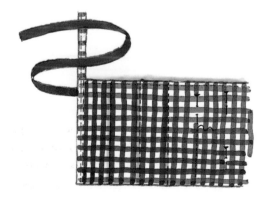

*3* Using pins, mark the positions of the cutlery pockets on the top edge of the loose hem, spacing them approximately 1½ in. (4cm) apart. Machine stitch vertical lines down the hem at each pin position to form the pockets. Insert the cutlery, fold over the top hem, roll up, and tie together with the cotton tapes.

# rabbit doll

## *you will need*

Calico for rabbit and pinafore

Striped fabric for dress

Synthetic toy stuffing

Templates on pages 142–143

Sewing machine

Needle and thread

Fine fiber-tipped pen

Scissors

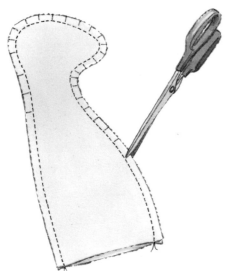

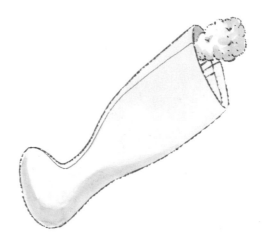

*1* Using the templates, cut out two bodies, four arms, four legs, and four ears from calico. Place the two bodies right sides together and stitch around the shaped edges, taking a ¼ in. (6mm) seam and leaving the straight bottom edges open. Snip into the curved seam allowances and turn right side out.

*2* Press the raw bottom edges of the body ¼ in. (6mm) to the wrong side. Start to stuff the head firmly with small pieces of toy stuffing. Continue stuffing until the body is filled and a good shape, then pin the lower pressed edges together to hold the stuffing in place.

*3* With right sides facing, stitch the arms together in pairs, taking a ¼ in. (6mm) seam and leaving the top straight edges open. Clip the curved seam allowances and turn right side out. Stuff each arm firmly with toy stuffing. Turn the top straight edges ¼ in. (6mm) to wrong side and stitch edges together to hold the stuffing in place.

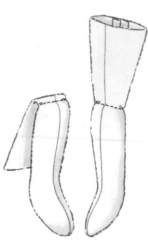

4 With right sides facing, stitch the legs together in pairs, taking a ¼ in. (6mm) seam and leaving the top straight edges open. Clip the curved seam allowances and turn to right side. Start to stuff each leg up to about the knee, then squash the legs flat, bringing the seams to lie on top of each other. Machine-stitch across each leg at the knee position to form the joint.

5 Remove the pins on each side of the body's lower edge and insert the top raw edge of each leg, making sure that both feet face toward the front. Pin in place and machine-stitch across the lower edge, catching the legs in place at the same time.

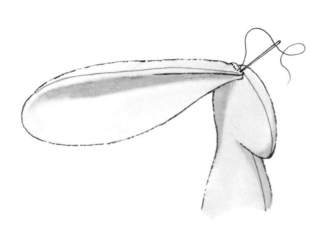

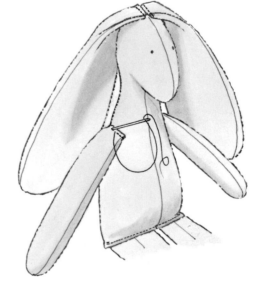

6 With right sides facing, stitch the ears together in pairs, taking a ¼ in. (6mm) seam and leaving the short straight edges open. Clip the curved seam allowances and turn right side out. Fold and press the short raw edges ¼ in. (6mm) to wrong side. Fold each ear in half at the short pressed edges and hand-stitch the folded ends to the top of the head each side of the seam.

7 Finally, hand-stitch the short straight ends of the arms to the sides of the body just below the neck and draw on two eyes using the fiber-tipped pen.

*8* Using the template, cut out two dresses from the striped fabric. With right sides facing, stitch the two dresses together along the over-arms and around the side seams. Press the sleeve raw edges and dress lower edge ¼ in. (6mm) to wrong side and stitch in place. Turn the dress right side out.

*9* Fold over a ¼ in. (6mm) hem to the wrong side around the neck edge. Put the dress onto the rabbit and work a row of gathering stitches around the neckline. Pull up the gathers to fit the neck and fasten off the thread.

*10* Using the templates, cut out two pinafore backs, one front, and two pockets from calico. With right sides facing, stitch the front pinafore to the backs along the shoulders and side seams. Press a ¼ in. (6mm) hem to the wrong side around all remaining raw edges and stitch hems in place.

*11* Press over a ⅜ in. (1cm) hem to wrong side on the top edges of the pockets and stitch in place. Press remaining raw edges to wrong sides and stitch pockets to front of pinafore. Fold three pleats at the front neck and stitch in place. Put the pinafore on to the rabbit over the dress and stitch the back edges together at the neck.

# fabric-covered box files

### *you will need*

Box file

Printed cotton fabric

Mount board the same size as box base, plus ⅛ in. (3mm) all around

Spray adhesive

White glue

Tape measure

24 in. (61cm) of ⅝-in. (1.5-cm) wide ribbon

Decorative lining paper

*1* For the top of the box measure and cut out a piece of fabric, the width of the lid, plus the depth of the box (A), by the length of the lid (B) and add a ⅝ in. (1.5cm) hem all around. For the front of the box measure and cut out a piece of fabric the length (C), by the depth (D), adding a ⅝ in. (1.5cm) hem all around. Finally, for the two sides measure and cut out two pieces of fabric the width (E), by the depth (F), adding a ⅝ in. (1.5cm) hem all around.

*2* Press over the hem allowance to the wrong side on both short edges of the side and front fabric pieces. Glue the pieces to the box using spray adhesive, folding the top hem allowances to the inside of the box and the lower hems around on to the base.

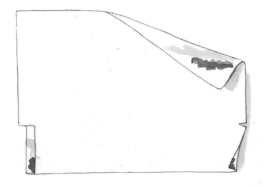

*3* On the top fabric piece measure up one of the shorter side edges, the hem allowance plus the depth of the box and make a ⅝ in. (1.5cm) horizontal snip into the fabric. Repeat on the opposite side edge and press the hem allowance below the snips to the wrong side.

*4* Glue the top piece of fabric to the box, lining up the pressed hem edges at the corners of the box and folding the lower hem on to the base. At the front two corners of the lid fold the hems back diagonally and then fold the remaining hems to the underside of the lid to create mitered corners.

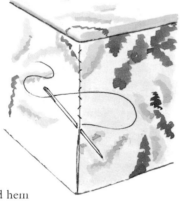

*5* Slipstitch the pressed hem edges together at each corner of the box.

*6* Cut the ribbon into two equal lengths, and using the white glue, stick the end of one length to the center front edge on the inside of the lid, and the other to base of the box to correspond. Leave to dry.

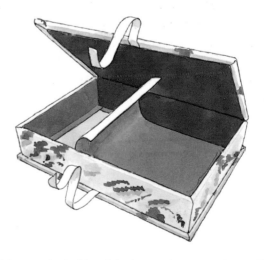

*7* Cut out a piece of fabric to fit the mount board, adding a ⅝ in. (1.5cm) hem all around. Using spray adhesive stick the fabric to the board, folding over the hems and mitering all four corners as shown in step 4 for the lid. Glue the board to the base of the box using white glue, sandwiching the ribbon tie in between.

*8* Measure the inside of the box and cut out pieces of decorative paper to line the inside. Stick the paper in place using the spray adhesive, making sure you cover all the raw hem edges.

# placemat

### *you will need*

Printed cotton fabric in two contrasting colors

Sewing machine

Needle and thread

Tape measure

Pins

Tray

*1* Measure the length and width of the tray base and add ¾ in. (2cm) to each measurement for seam allowances. Cut out a rectangle from each of the printed fabrics to these measurements.

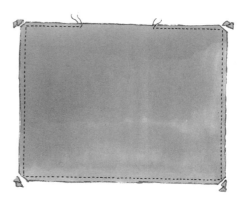

*2* With right sides together, pin and then machine stitch the two pieces of fabric together around the outer edges, taking a ⅜ in. (1cm) seam and leaving a 4 in. (10cm) opening along one short side. Cut diagonally across the seam turnings at each corner to reduce the bulk.

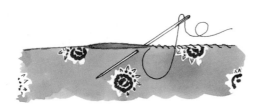

*3* Turn the placemat right side out. Press seamed edges flat and opening edges ⅜ in. (1cm) to wrong side. Slipstitch the opening edges closed.

*4* Thread up your sewing machine with a different colored thread in the needle and on the bobbin, to match the two contrasting fabrics of your placemat, then top stitch around all sides, working close to the edge.

# fabric-covered coat hanger

### *you will need*

Vintage cotton or linen fabric

Needle and thread

Wooden clothes hanger

Tailor's chalk

Scissors

Tape measure

Pins

Two buttons (optional)

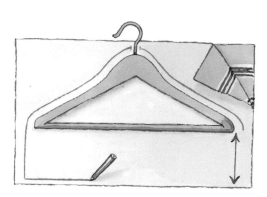

*1* Place the coat hanger on to the wrong side of the fabric and draw around the top edge with tailor's chalk, marking the position of the hook at the top. Extend the chalk line down vertically from each side of the hanger for about 4 in. (10cm) and join the ends together with a straight line to form the lower edge of the cover. Cut out two shapes from fabric adding a ⅝ in. (1.5cm) seam/hem allowance all around.

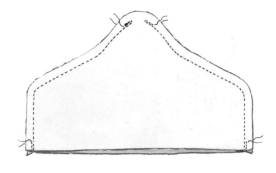

*2* With right sides facing, stitch the two fabric pieces together around the top shaped edges, taking a ⅝ in. (1.5cm) seam and leaving a ⅜ in. (1cm) opening at the hook position.

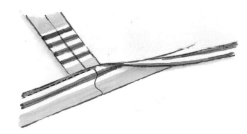

*3* Along the lower edge of the cover, turn over a ⅜ in. (1cm) double hem and stitch in place by hand or machine. Turn the cover right side out and press the seamed edges flat.

*4* Insert the coat hanger, then either stitch on two buttons to the top outer edges of the cover, or sew on bows made from the same fabric to prevent garment loops slipping off the hanger.

# pencil cups

### *you will need*

Paper for making templates
Pencil and ruler
Scissors
Felted/boiled wool sweater
Needle and strong thread

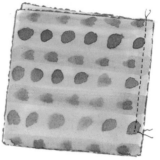

*2* With wrong sides facing stitch two felted wool pieces together down one edge, taking a ¼ in. (6mm) seam and finishing ¼ in. (6mm) from the lower edge. Repeat to join four of the pieces together into a ring.

*1* For the square pencil cup draw and cut out a template 4 in. (10cm) square from the paper. Cut out five pieces of felted wool using the template.

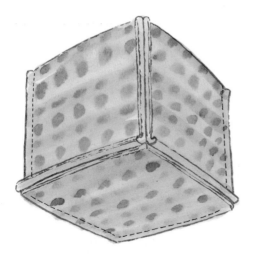

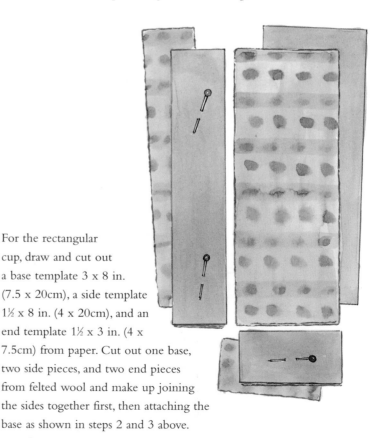

*4* For the rectangular cup, draw and cut out a base template 3 x 8 in. (7.5 x 20cm), a side template 1½ x 8 in. (4 x 20cm), and an end template 1½ x 3 in. (4 x 7.5cm) from paper. Cut out one base, two side pieces, and two end pieces from felted wool and make up joining the sides together first, then attaching the base as shown in steps 2 and 3 above.

*3* Stitch the remaining piece to the lower edge of the ring, matching corners to seams and taking a ¼ in. (6mm) seam allowance, to form the base.

# templates

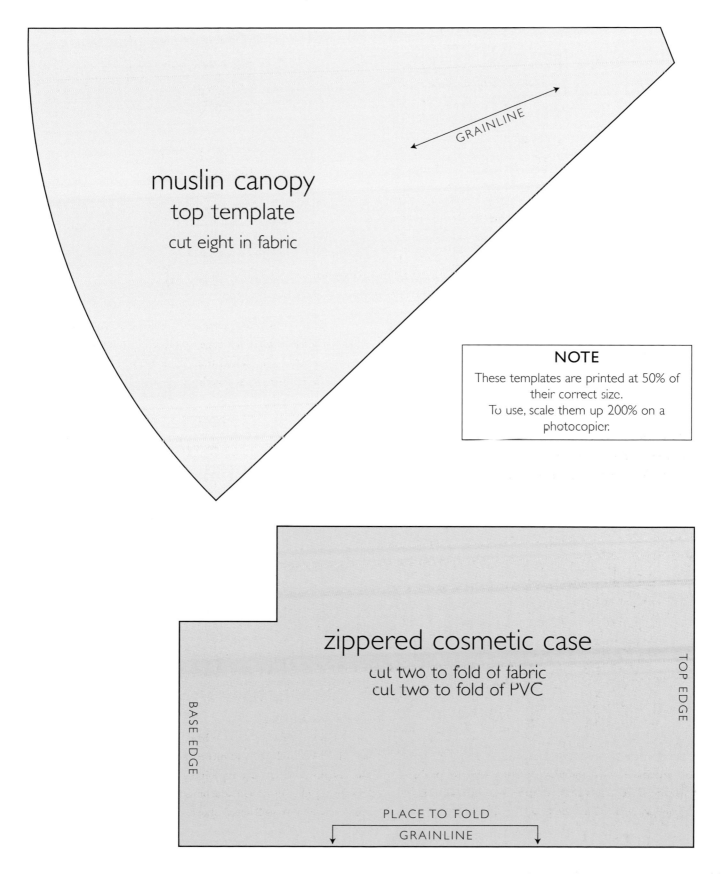

GRAINLINE

## muslin canopy
### top template
cut eight in fabric

**NOTE**

These templates are printed at 50% of their correct size.
To use, scale them up 200% on a photocopier.

## zippered cosmetic case
cut two to fold of fabric
cut two to fold of PVC

BASE EDGE

TOP EDGE

PLACE TO FOLD

GRAINLINE

**NOTE**

These templates are printed at 50% of their correct size. To use, scale them up 200% on a photocopier.

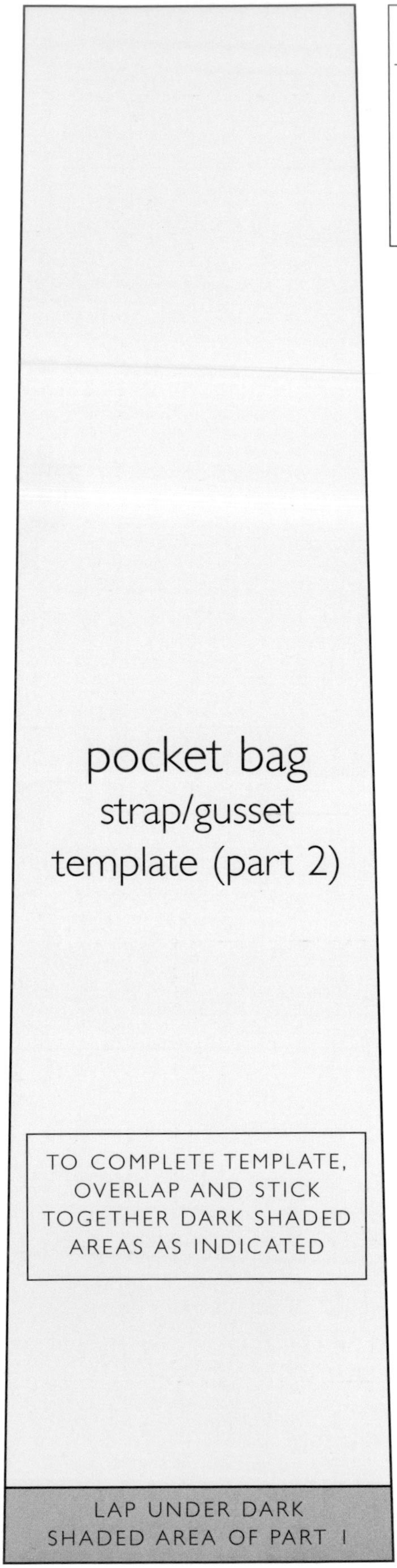

LAP OVER DARK SHADED
AREA OF PART 2

GRAINLINE

pocket bag
strap/gusset
template (part 2)

pocket bag
strap/gusset template
(part 1)

cut two from canvas
cut two from printed fabric

TO COMPLETE TEMPLATE,
OVERLAP AND STICK
TOGETHER DARK SHADED
AREAS AS INDICATED

LAP UNDER DARK
SHADED AREA OF PART 1

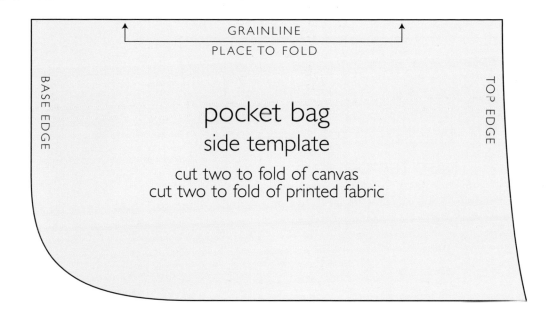

GRAINLINE
PLACE TO FOLD

BASE EDGE

TOP EDGE

# pocket bag
## side template

cut two to fold of canvas
cut two to fold of printed fabric

---

### NOTE

These templates are printed at 50% of their correct size.
To use, scale them up 200% on a photocopier.

---

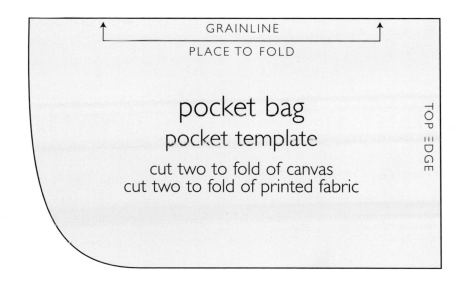

GRAINLINE
PLACE TO FOLD

# pocket bag
## pocket template

cut two to fold of canvas
cut two to fold of printed fabric

TOP EDGE

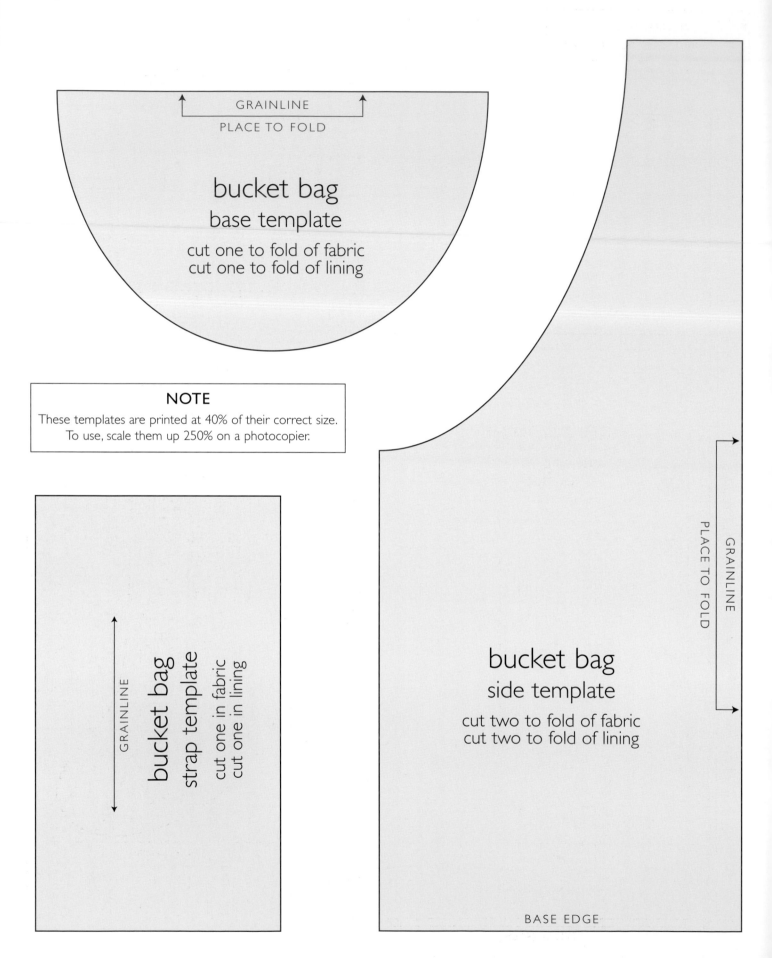

GRAINLINE
PLACE TO FOLD

# bucket bag
## base template

cut one to fold of fabric
cut one to fold of lining

**NOTE**
These templates are printed at 40% of their correct size.
To use, scale them up 250% on a photocopier.

GRAINLINE

bucket bag
strap template

cut one in fabric
cut one in lining

PLACE TO FOLD

GRAINLINE

# bucket bag
## side template

cut two to fold of fabric
cut two to fold of lining

BASE EDGE

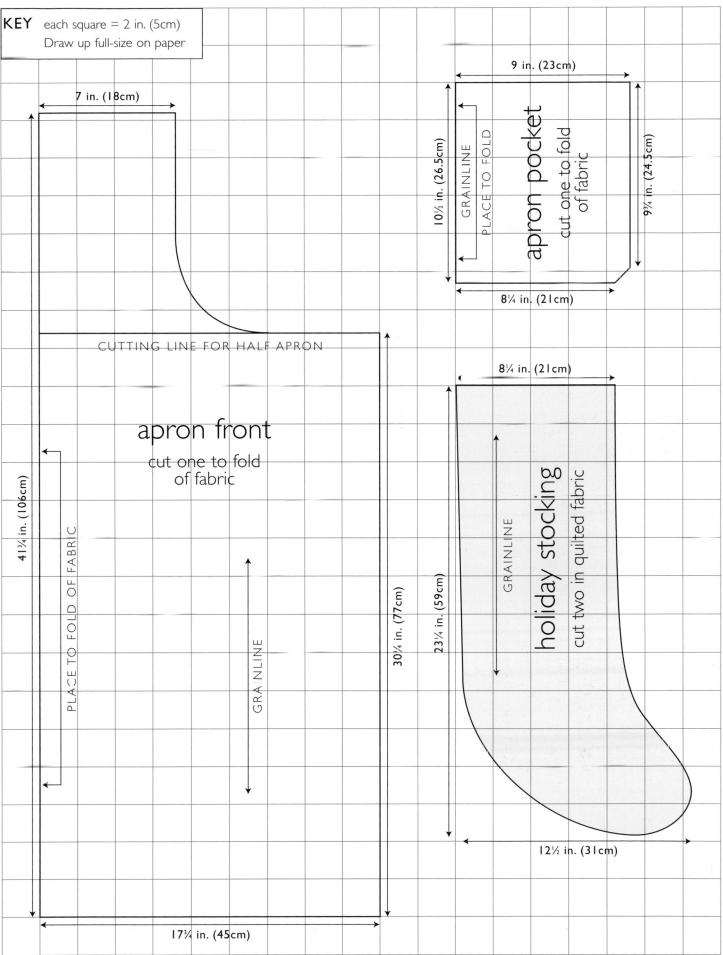

KEY each square = 2 in. (5cm)
Draw up full-size on paper

7 in. (18cm)

CUTTING LINE FOR HALF APRON

apron front

cut one to fold
of fabric

41¾ in. (106cm)

PLACE TO FOLD OF FABRIC

GRAINLINE

30¼ in. (77cm)

17¾ in. (45cm)

9 in. (23cm)

10½ in. (26.5cm)

GRAINLINE

PLACE TO FOLD

apron pocket

cut one to fold
of fabric

9¾ in. (24.5cm)

8¼ in. (21cm)

8¼ in. (21cm)

23¼ in. (59cm)

GRAINLINE

holiday stocking

cut two in quilted fabric

12½ in. (31cm)

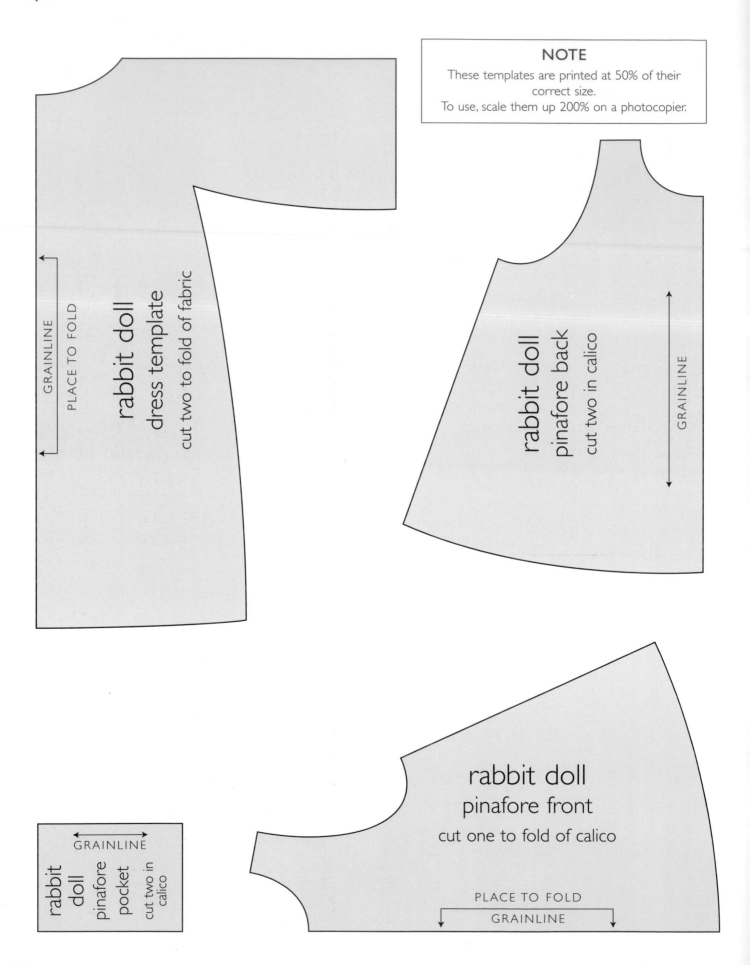

**NOTE**

These templates are printed at 50% of their correct size.
To use, scale them up 200% on a photocopier.

GRAINLINE

PLACE TO FOLD

**rabbit doll**
dress template
cut two to fold of fabric

**rabbit doll**
pinafore back
cut two in calico

GRAINLINE

**rabbit doll**
pinafore front
cut one to fold of calico

PLACE TO FOLD
GRAINLINE

GRAINLINE

rabbit doll pinafore pocket
cut two in calico

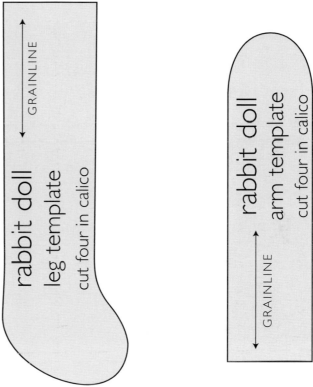

**NOTE**

These templates are printed at 50% of their correct size.
To use, scale them up 200% on a photocopier.

rabbit doll
body template
cut two in calico

GRAINLINE

rabbit doll
leg template
cut four in calico

GRAINLINE

rabbit doll
arm template
cut four in calico

GRAINLINE

GRAINLINE

rabbit doll

ear template

cut four in calico

# index

# author's acknowledgments

There are many people to whom I owe thanks for their help in making this book, not least my mother Mary Amoroso-Centeno who was willing and not a little eager to assist in making some of the projects, even at the age of 84 with a part-time job in a charity shop and a full and busy life.

To my daughter Kate, who helped conjure up some of the ideas and made a scrapbook to prove to me (when I was very, very reluctant) that a sewing book could indeed be beautiful. She also kindly modeled in some of the photographs for no reward other than an apron.

To Tina Wright, who was there in my biggest panic and taught me how to use a sewing machine.

To Penny Menato, who worked quickly and with little notice to provide emergency projects at the last minute.

To Jane Bolsover who explained in an expert way exactly how to make the projects, Kate Simunek who created beautiful illustrations, and Christine Wood for her wonderful design.

To Lucinda Symons, who made beautiful photographs, assisted by Cesca Sims and Spencer Murphy, and who was such a pleasure to work with.

To Amanda Austin, who is the cleverest florist in London and whose shop across the road from Cabbages & Roses was willing and happy to provide flowers and advice.

And last but not least, my thanks to Cindy Richards and Gillian Haslam for their faith in me.

# stockists

*Contact the Cabbages & Roses website for details of suppliers of their fabrics:*

www.cabbagesandroses.com

*Or visit their shop at:*
3 Langton Street
London SW10 0JL
Telephone: 020 7352 7333